Sitting on God's Lap... *Listening*

More Meditations about The Invisible Presence

By Eleanor Isaacson

Copyright © 2021 by Eleanor Isaacson

Scripture quotations are from The ESV® Bible (The Holy Bible, English Standard Version®), copyright © 2001 by Crossway, a publishing ministry of Good News Publishers. Used by permission. All rights reserved.

Eleanor Isaacson Publications
https://www.eleanorisaacson.com

Eleanor Isaacson Publications

ISBN 978-0-9991374-2-0

Book and E-book designed and formatted by EBook Listing Services
www.ebooklistingservices.com

Cover designed by Larissa Design
www.behance.net/larissadesign

The cover image has been designed with a photo from Freepik.com.

1 3 5 7 9 10 8 6 4 2
Printed in the United States of America

Sitting on God's Lap... *Listening*

ISAIAH 55:3

A Special Note
from an Olde Order Amish Family

Eleanor and our family share a common bond that is our German background and culture. We also share the love of God and His Word. Eleanor is truly a gift from God to all of us. Her love for the Lord and the Bible and her joyful positive spirit make her an amazing woman. We need her in our lives and we thank God for having brought her to all of us. We all love her and she has become a part of our families.

We feel so very blest to know you Eleanor. You are a wonderful gift from God to us, and we have learned to know you and love you. We so appreciate your interest in our lives! May the Lord be honored and glorified as we continue to serve Him and may our friendship continue to grow for a long time.

~RJE

Dedication

I dedicate this book to all the people I have mentored, guided, discipled, influenced, prayed over, loved like my children, listened to, worried about, taught the Bible to and lived before them.

Hoping I did it all the right way for you to be encouraged.

Wishing all of you God's very best in your life's journey.

Love 'ya lots always

Eleanor

Foreword
by Dr. Chris Walker
Senior Pastor,
Westminster Presbyterian Church

A fellow pastor once told me that the central task of any church is to determine how it is going to fulfill Jesus' Great Commission to make disciples of all nations. But as a church, we know that the gospel doesn't go out through an organizational system. It goes out when the people in our church are faithful to talk about Jesus and his salvation and to disciple others to grow in their faith. And Eleanor Isaacson has been just such a person in our church.

One of the first things that will strike anyone about Eleanor is the energy and enthusiasm she has for talking about Jesus and about the Bible. When I started as the youth pastor at Westminster Presbyterian Church, Eleanor was a volunteer helper with our youth group. She shared her testimony of God's salvation in Jesus, invited girls over to her home, and mentored teens in our youth group, some of whom she is still in contact with years later.

But Eleanor's efforts weren't confined to discipling teens and adults in the church. She has used her striking story of God rescuing her from Hitler's Germany as an open door to share the gospel of salvation through faith in Jesus in many different circles. She has made herself available to mentor and encourage woman throughout the county, always bringing them back to God's word and encouraging them to find their hope in Scripture and its offer of salvation in Christ.

As a pastor, I am thankful that God uses his people as ambassadors for Christ, and I'm thankful that he has given our church and our county a faithful ambassador in Eleanor Isaacson.

—Dr. Chris Walker, Senior Pastor
Westminster Presbyterian Church
Lancaster, PA

Acknowledgements

I wish to acknowledge all the people, friends, colleagues and associates, with whom I served on boards and committees throughout my life. Your friendships encouraged me over the years to move forward in all my pursuits, both in New Jersey and in Pennsylvania. Thank you for everything I learned, both positive and negative, through my association with all of you. Wishing you all the best in life as you move forward in your journey.

THANK YOU TO MY WONDERFUL FRIENDS

Sharon and Chet Beiler
Dee Boonstra
Gentine and Geoff Clark
Carol Fausel
Jordan and Amy Hostetter
Ruthie and Scott Keating
Arlene and Charlie Kreider

Betsy Prothero
Laura Schanz
Jan Schutzky
Tami and Mark Swaim
Anne Marie and David Teply
Jeanette Windle
Barbara Zagier

PLACES IN NEW JERSEY

Kenilworth Chapel
Mountain Ridge Chapel
Long Hill Chapel
Willow Grove Church
Northeastern Bible College
    served as president of the Auxiliary
    taught Bible studies

Fairly Dickinson University
    graduated magna cum laude
St. Barnabas Hospital
    Auxiliary Board
Elizabethtown Gas Company
    served as assistant to the President
Mutual of Omaha
    Insurance agent—#2 female agent in the USA 1985
John Robert Powers School
Barbizon School
    served as Director of Admissions
    Instructor in Personal Improvement
    Fashion Model
Voice Teachers and Coaches
Ballroom Dance Instructors

PLACES IN PENNSYLVANIA

Lancaster General Hospital Committees
Willow Valley Committees
Lancaster Symphony Committees
Women's Symphony - Board
Lancaster Bible College
    served on committees
Dayspring Christian Academy Committee
Monterey Chapel
Lancaster Art Association - Board
Rabbi Green and Family
Millersville University
    Mentoring Program
Westminster Presbyterian Church PCA

A Special Thank-You

A special thank you to Amy Deardon at Ebook Listing Services (www.ebooklistingservices.com).

Her gentle way of encouraging me to write has been the source of my keeping on the path of creating more books.

Her skill and expertise in editing, formatting, and typesetting has not only been inspiring but it has given me the confidence and courage to pursue my own skill in writing.

Amy, thank you for your faithful service to many dormant writers who need to be connected with you.

Table of Contents

Do You Want to Know God?

When you think about it, all belief systems including atheism teach that humans can, by their own efforts, work hard to become worthy to be with God (or to become a good person).

The only belief system that contradicts this idea of the inherent goodness of people is the system centering around Jesus Christ. So right there, since it stands alone, it's worth understanding how and why being a believer is so different from all other systems.

God is unimaginably Holy and Perfect. No human can possibly be "good enough" to be with Him.

> For all have sinned, and fall short of the glory of God.
>
> —Romans 3:23

No matter how hard you try to be "worthy" (however that looks to you) you will never be able to do this perfectly. If you break God's moral law only one time that is enough to separate you permanently. Have you ever stolen anything, even something small? Have you ever lied? Have you ever pursued something or someone that didn't belong to you?

> For whoever keeps the whole law but fails in one point has become guilty of all of it.
>
> —James 2:10

However there is Good News! God is also infinitely Love... He IS love, not just HAS love. He deeply longs for each person to be reconciled to Himself, and therefore makes a way.

> For the wages of sin is death, but the free gift of God is eternal life in Christ Jesus our Lord.
>
> —Romans 6:23

The cornerstone of belief in Jesus is John 3:16:

For God so loved the world, that he gave his only begotten Son, that whoever believes in him shall not perish but have eternal life.

—John 3:16

Who is Jesus?

He was a real person, a Jewish man born of the line of Abrahan, Judah and David, who lived and died in Israel in the first century A.D.

Believers in Jesus also say he is the Son of God, God's perfect sacrificial lamb. Jesus lived without sin and freely offered his life so that through His sacrifice, we might be saved from condemnation and declared righteous and cleansed from sin before a holy God.

When you trust that Jesus paid the price for your sins, you can be reconciled to God:

There is therefore now no condemnation for those who are in Christ Jesus...

—Romans 8:1

God simply wants you to turn to Him and humbly trust him Him rather than trying to do it yourself. If you want to follow Him your words don't matter so much as your attitude. You can pray something like this:

Lord Jesus, I want to know You personally. Thank You for dying on the cross for my sins. I open the door of my life and receive You as my Savior and Lord. Thank You for forgiving me of my sins and giving me eternal life. Take control of the throne of my life. Make me the kind of person You want me to be.*

*prayer from Bill Bright's The Four Spiritual Laws (http://www.umich.edu/~mpactmov/4laws.htm)

If you confess with your mouth that Jesus is Lord and believe in your heart that God raised him from the dead, you will be saved.

—Romans 10:9

If you have prayed that prayer, you are in! Ask God to guide you as you learn more about Him.

Read your Bible starting with the book of John—this is the fourth book in the New Testament.

Find other believers. Feel free to write to me on my website at www.eleanorisaacson.com if you have questions.

Welcome to the family!

So What Do You Think?

_____

_____

_____

_____

_____

_____

_____

_____

_____

_____

_____

_____

_____

_____

_____

_____

_____

_____

_____

_____

_____

God—Our Eternal Husband
Singleness is a Special Gift from God

For your Maker is your husband, the Lord of hosts is his name; and the Holy One of Israel is your Redeemer...

—Isaiah 54:5

For I feel a divine jealousy for you, since I betrothed you to one husband, to present you as a pure virgin to Christ.

—2 Corinthians 11:2

And I will betroth you to me forever. I will betroth you to me in righteousness and in justice, in steadfast love and in mercy. I will betroth you to me in faithfulness. And you shall know the Lord.

—Hosea 2:19-20

So you're single, widowed, divorced! All your friends are married. You feel left out, wondering if God is mad at you. No, He isn't mad at you.

In Ecclesiastes 3:1-8 we read that there is a time and season for everything: to be born and to die, to plant and to pluck up that which is planted, to kill and to heal, and so forth.

So if you are one in a world of twos, make it a spiritual journey. Your singleness may not be forever. Use it to dig deeper into the *Love of God* for you. This will help you wait patiently for Mr./Mrs. Right, if that is God's will for you, but if not, your faith will grow into God and you will perhaps become even a more useful person to Him.

How did Adam find his mate? Did he join all sorts of clubs to meet somebody? No... He slept in the Will of God!

So the Lord is our husband. What exactly does that mean in our single lives? Well, the Lord as a husband provides for us, loves us, shelters us, understands us, gives us children (spiritual ones), and wants us to believe how much He loves us.

For the Lord Jesus to die for us to make us His Bride is beyond any human comprehension.

How do we lay hold of that truth? We need to focus on all the promises about his abiding Presence with us, and look up all the verses daily to make them all sink into our soul.

Here are some verses for you:

As the Father has loved me, so have I loved you...

—John 15:9

...I will never leave you nor forsake you.

—Hebrews 13:5

For you were bought with a price...

—1 Corinthians 6:20

His left hand is under my head, and his right hand embraces me.

—Song of Solomon 2:6

So my friend, you are so loved. If God has a special earthly love for you, wait His time and He will give you the Best.

Indeed, none who wait for you shall be put to shame...

—Psalm 25:3

So What Do You Think?

_____

_____

_____

_____

_____

_____

_____

_____

_____

_____

_____

_____

_____

_____

_____

_____

_____

_____

_____

_____

_____

What Are Your Plans?

...and behold, the bush was burning, yet it was not consumed.

—Exodus 3:2

At eighty years of age, Moses began his greatest ministry AFTER the fire went out. At this point in his life, he had no more self confidence, no agenda, no goals, no dreams for his future. He was just a blank piece of paper available to let God write His plan on it.

Moses learned for the first forty years of his life to be Somebody. Then he had to learn for the next forty years to be Nobody. Now at eighty God could use him because all his ambitions were out of the way. So it is with us. You want to make God laugh? Just tell him your plans and give Him your agenda.

Interesting, when Moses saw that burning bush, he did not stay and pray or build an altar, after the fire went out, to commemorate this exciting event. Neither did he break off branches to bring home to the little woman or neighbors to show off and ultimately worship it. Remember, the Israelites worshipped the Snake on the Pole long after the actual miracle. (2 Kings 18) It was Hezekiah who called the snake "*Nehushtan.*" The people worshiped it and burned incense to it. Hezekiah destroyed it.

No, Moses immediately obeyed the voice of the Lord, with fear and trembling. He stuttered. Maybe he had had a stroke somewhere along the way.

Now at eighty, he was ready to rely wholly on the Lord for the next forty years to serve the Lord and His people. The words of the Lord, "I will be with you" (Exodus 3:12), gave him all the confidence he needed to do the job, and not lose heart when the tests came, and to move forward. He could have never done all he did forty years earlier. Even if he had, he probably would have been too proud of it all rather than focusing on God.

So it is with us. It is when we are broken that God can use us. When we have lost confidence in our abilities, experiences and knowledge of who we are, that we become a clean slate for God to use us as well.

So dear believer, if you are being pruned right now and God is stripping you, be assured it is to make you a sharp instrument and a clean vessel. It has been said "God is never more near than when He is pruning you." (see John 15:2).

So What Do You Think?

_____
_____
_____
_____
_____
_____
_____
_____
_____
_____
_____
_____
_____
_____
_____
_____
_____
_____

Am I Not Enough For Thee?

Am I not enough, mine own?
Enough, mine own, for thee?
Hath the world its palace towers,
   garden glades of magic flowers,
   where thou fain wouldst be?

Fair things and false are there,
   False things but fair.
All shalt thou find at last,
   only in me.
Am I not enough mine own?
I, for ever and alone,
   I, needing thee?

—Gerhard Tersteegen(1697-1769)

11

So What Do You Think?

_____

_____

_____

_____

_____

_____

_____

_____

_____

_____

_____

_____

_____

_____

_____

_____

_____

_____

_____

_____

God's Back Parts

You cannot see my face, for man shall not see me and live...Behold, there is a place by me where you shall stand on the rock... and I will cover you with my hand until I have passed by. Then I will take away my hand, and you shall see my back, but my face shall not be seen.

—Exodus 33:20-23

It was not until our Lord Jesus came upon the scene that we could actually "see" the face of God in Him. His eternal glory was veiled in human flesh, but many saw glimpses of it on occasion during His ministry. In the Old Testament though, God was hiding Himself until Christ the Messiah came.

So what can we glean from all this? Well, in our daily lives, with its joys and sorrows, trials and victories, He comes and comes to us, and during a crisis he keeps on coming, but He hides Himself from our view until the crisis has passed. Then we look back and see "how" the Lord was with us all the time. We see His hand in it all, and thank and praise Him for it. We also grow in our faith after a trial. I know I have, and I am sure you have too.

So the silent years in our lives are an important part of our spiritual growth. We can't see Him coming in a crisis, but you will know when it is over that He was with you all the time.

Nice isn't it? So don't panic when the bottom falls out. You are standing on a firm foundation when you know His love for you. Our Lord Jesus Christ is a firm foundation at all times.

In a crisis, do you go to the Throne or to the Phone?

So What Do You Think?

Wisdom

At Gibeon the Lord appeared to Solomon in a dream by night, and God said, "Ask what I shall give you."

And Solomon said, "You have shown great and steadfast love to your servant David my father, because he walked before you in faithfulness, in righteousness, and in uprightness of heart toward you. And you have kept for him this great and steadfast love and have given him a son to sit on his throne this day.

And now, O Lord my God, you have made your servant king in place of David my father, although I am but a little child. I do not know how to go out or come in.

And your servant is in the midst of your people whom you have chosen, a great people, too many to be numbered or counted for multitude.

Give your servant therefore an understanding mind to govern your people, that I may discern between good and evil, for who is able to govern this your great people?"

It pleased the Lord that Solomon had asked this.

And God said to him, "Because you have asked this, and have not asked for yourself long life or riches or the life of your enemies, but have asked for yourself understanding to discern what is right...I give you also what you have not asked, both riches and honor, so that no other king shall compare with you, all your days."

—1 Kings 3:5-11, 13

King Solomon prayed for wisdom to govern the people of God, and God answered him almost instantly.

God was pleased with Solomon's request and because he did not ask for riches and honor, God gave him all the riches of the then world anyway. Right after this we see that God immediately answered Solomon's prayer for wisdom. The two harlots came to him with their babies, one alive and the other dead. They were fighting about which baby was the mother of the living baby. Naturally the mother of the living baby said *"No! Let's not kill it. Let her have it"* (1 Kings 3:26). What wisdom!

What is sad about Solomon is that he never asked God for wisdom to control his private life. His sexuality controlled him and ultimately destroyed him and the nation of Israel. He had seven-hundred wives and three-hundred concubines. His three-hundred concubines were used to bear children and for sexual pleasure. Solomon's seven-hundred wives were foreign women and princesses, one of whom was Pharaoh's daughter. He acquired women of Moab, Ammon, Edom, Sidon and Hittites. The purpose of him marrying these women was to maintain peace in the region. His lack of discipline and control ultimately destroyed him and the whole nation.

Why was he so loose about women? Well, he learned it all from his father, David, who had four wives and thirty concubines. David was not disciplined about that subject either. I'm sure he must have been thinking *"I am the king, I can do as I please. My private life is my business."* Well, the example he set for his children was a bad one.

So what can we learn from all this? Children watch us—our lives, attitudes, and behaviors. They imitate us and usually go beyond us of what we did. The key is to not imitate the sinful lifestyle of our parents and friends, but to commit our body, soul and spirit to the Lord BEFORE we are face to face with temptations.

> But as for you, O man of God, flee these things. Pursue righteousness, godliness, faith, love, steadfastness, gentleness.
>
> —1 Timothy 6:11

> ...which is why I suffer as I do. But I am not ashamed, for I know whom I have believed, and I am convinced that he is able to guard until that day what has been entrusted to me.
>
> —2 Timothy 1:12

So What Do You Think?

_____

_____

_____

_____

_____

_____

_____

_____

_____

_____

_____

_____

_____

_____

_____

_____

_____

_____

_____

_____

_____

Peter Walked on Water

But immediately Jesus spoke to them, saying, "Take heart; it is I. Do not be afraid." And Peter answered him, "Lord, if it is you, command me to come to you on the water." Jesus said, "Come." So Peter got out of the boat and walked on the water and came to Jesus. But when Peter saw the wind, he was afraid, and beginning to sink he cried out, "Lord, save me." Jesus immediately reached out his hand and took hold of him, saying to him, "O you of little faith, why did you doubt?"

—Matthew 14:27-31

Yes, Peter actually did walk on water, even though it may have been just a few seconds. How could he do that? He was a human being and, let's face it, we humans just don't walk on water unless it is frozen—ice!

So how could Peter actually walk on water toward the Lord Jesus Christ? It is because the Word of the Lord is a strong foundation, a Rock:

> Psalm 18:2: The Lord is my Rock…
> Psalm 31:3: For Thou art my Rock and my fortress...
> Psalm 62:2: He only is my rock and my salvation…
> Psalm 94:22: My God is the rock of my refuge…
> 1 Corinthians 10:4: And that Rock was Christ…

When Peter kept his focus on *Who Christ was*, it kept him above the waves. Looking at his surroundings, he fell. But Peter, unlike the others, was bold, curious and wanted to test his faith. He learned more than all the other disciples.

How very much like us! When we keep our focus on *Who the Lord is* and *what He has done for us*, we are also kept above the waves. It is when our problems become bigger than God that we fall apart.

For he knows our frame; he remembers that we are dust.

—Psalm 103:14

Even when we fall, like Peter did, the Lord rescues us because He knows our frame and remembers that we are but dust. How loving and gracious our God is! Let us praise Him.

So What Do You Think?

_____

_____

_____

_____

_____

_____

_____

_____

_____

_____

_____

_____

_____

_____

_____

_____

_____

_____

_____

_____

God Identifies with Us in Every Way
Even in Our Environment

Make a list of all the ways God identifies with us:

In the Human Kingdom

- He became a baby (Luke 2:1-20).
- He grew up as a man (Luke 2:40-52).
- He is a shepherd (Psalm 23).
- He is our Husband (Isaiah 54:5).
- He is a father (Matthew 6:9) and a son (John 11:4).
- He is our brother (Hebrews 2:11-15).
- He is our guide in life (Psalm 48:14).
- He is our bridegroom (Revelation 19:7).
- He is our King (Psalm 47:6-7).
- He is our High Priest (Hebrews 4:14-16).
- He is our Physician (Psalm 147:3).
- He is our Living Bread (John 6:51).
- He is our Living Water (John 7:38).
- He is the Light (1 John 1:5).
- He is the Way (John 14:6).
- He is the Truth (John 14:6).
- He is the Life (John 14:6).
- He is our Judge (Isaiah 33:22).
- He is our Substitute (John 1:29).
- He is the door (John 10:7).
- He is the Resurrection (John 11:25).
- He is our forerunner (Hebrews 6:20).
- He is our Master (Romans 6:22).

In the Animal Kingdom

- He is the Lion (Hosea 5:14; Revelation 5:5).
- He is the Lamb (John 1:29).

In the Vegetable Kingdom

- He is the Vine (John 15:5).
- He is the Lily of the Valley (Song of Solomon 2:1).
- He is the Rose of Sharon (Song of Solomon 2:1).
- He is the Branch (Isaiah 11:1).

In the Mineral Kingdom

- He is the Rock of Ages (Isaiah 26:4).
- His words are more precious than refined gold (Psalm 19:10) and silver (Psalm 12:6).

You may want to add to this list. Make it a part of your devotions.

So What Do You Think?

_____

_____

_____

_____

_____

_____

_____

_____

_____

_____

_____

_____

_____

_____

_____

_____

_____

_____

_____

_____

_____

Prayer

> Then Pharaoh called Moses and Aaron and said, "Plead with the Lord to take away the frogs from me and from my people, and I will let the people go to sacrifice to the Lord."
>
> Moses said to Pharaoh, "Be pleased to command me when I am to plead for you and for your servants and for your people, that the frogs be cut off from you and your houses and be left only in the Nile."
>
> And Pharaoh said, "Tomorrow."
>
> Moses said, "Be it as you say, so that you may know that there is no one like the Lord our God."
>
> —Exodus 8:8-10

Only one more night with the frogs!

Why were the frogs removed "tomorrow?" Why not now, today? God could have instantly removed the frogs at the word of Moses.

This might draw an example for us today. Could it be that we sometimes get comfortable with a problem or an illness?

> One man was there who had been an invalid for thirty-eight years. When Jesus saw him lying there and knew that he had already been there a long time, he said to him, "Do you want to be healed?"
>
> —John 5:5-6

I used to be surprised at the words of Jesus when He asked the paralyzed man *"Do you want to be healed?"* before He actually restored him.

Now that I'm older in my walk with the Lord, I am not surprised. Some people just don't want to get well. They can actually enjoy their illness and problems because it gives them power over family members and friends. Everybody fusses over them. They become the center of attention… and they love it! This might all end if the healing were to take place.

So our Lord Jesus, being the Gentlemen that He is, asks us for permission, I guess, to heal us. Are we bold to let Him bless us so that we can serve Him in a better way?

> Let us then with confidence draw near to the throne of grace, that we may receive mercy and find grace to help in time of need.
>
> —Hebrews 4:16

Sometimes our illness and problems help us focus on our lives and drives us to seek help from the Lord.

> Before I was afflicted I went astray, but now I keep your word.
>
> —Psalm 119:67

We need to be open and honest with Him who loves us and really understands us, and is ready to heal us in every way.

So What Do You Think?

_____

_____

_____

_____

_____

_____

_____

_____

_____

_____

_____

_____

_____

_____

_____

_____

_____

_____

_____

Forgiveness

...Father, forgive them; for they know not what they do...

—Luke 23:34

When the Lord Jesus Christ was on the cross this was the only place in Scripture where he asked His Father to forgive sinners.

Jesus Christ spoke forgiveness of people's sins throughout His earthly ministry. So why was it that when He paid the price for our sins on the Cross of Calvary, He asked His Father to forgive those who nailed Him there? Why did He not do it Himself?

Interesting question isn't it?

I think it was because when Jesus was hanging on that Cross, He was there not as the Son of God, but as a sinner—like you and me. During those hours, God the Father poured out all His wrath against sin upon our Lord Jesus. He was our substitute.

What Love, what Grace, for Him to be there willingly in our place!

But God shows his love for us in that while we were still sinners, Christ died for us.

—Romans 5:8

He died on the cross for the sins of the whole world once and for all:

He is the propitiation for our sins, and not for ours only but also for the sins of the whole world.

—1 John 2:2

...but as it is, he has appeared once for all at the end of the ages to put away sin by the sacrifice of himself.

—Hebrews 9:26

The Bible says in John 10:11: "*I am the good shepherd. The good shepherd lays down his life for the sheep.*" That's you and me!

How perfect is the Word of God to tell us about Jesus! During Jesus' life on this earth, He was the Perfect Man and the Perfect Son of God. During the crucifixion, he laid aside His Deity and became "a Sinner." He paid the price for our redemption.

When you say: "*I accept Jesus into my life and believe that He died for me, I have Eternal Life, I am a born again believer. I am accepted in Him by a Holy God, because my sins have been paid for,*" then you become part of God's family.

To the praise of his glorious grace, with which he has blessed us in the Beloved.

—Ephesians 1:6

Praise God....Hallelujah! What a Savior!

So if you have never opened your heart to Jesus Christ, why not do it today and begin a whole new life in Him. I did this February 25, 1954 at 8:45 a.m. and it was a Thursday!

What blessings have been in my life because of my decision years ago.

So What Do You Think?

_____

_____

_____

_____

_____

_____

_____

_____

_____

_____

_____

_____

_____

_____

_____

_____

_____

_____

_____

_____

Can Believers be Separated from God's Love?

Who shall separate us from the love of Christ? Shall tribulation, or distress, or persecution, or famine, or nakedness, or danger, or sword?

... No, in all these things we are more than conquerors through him who loved us.

For I am sure that neither death nor life, nor angels nor rulers, nor things present nor things to come, nor powers, nor height nor depth, nor anything else in all creation, will be able to separate us from the love of God in Christ Jesus our Lord.

—Romans 8:35, 37-39

No, believers can't be separated from the love of God, but as believers we may have a problem believing and receiving His Love.

In this passage from Romans what a long list of things that cannot separate us from the Love of God! But there is one thing left out of that list, and that is…OUR PAST.

I have counseled people young and old for more than 50 years, and it has amazed me how many people, who know Jesus Christ as Father, Friend and Savior, can't seem to believe that God really loves them. They have a problem receiving His Love. They know the Calvary Love Story, but they can't make it all personal. Why?

Sometimes the pain of the past—neglect, trauma, abandonment, violence and abuse—so consume our daily lives and thoughts as adults, that we just can't let go of it. Many adults connect their abusive fathers with the way God must be. So, how can the Love of God penetrate into that hurting soul? By lots of prayer, counsel, love, understanding, nurturing, discipling, accepting, perseverance and patience. With the help of the Holy Spirit and lots of love, it can penetrate into our lives.

So how can we shut ourselves off from receiving His Love? We shut ourselves off by being so consumed with our hurtful past. How can we be free from it? By making it all a part of our Spiritual Journey. If God allowed it in our lives, there must be something good in it for us. How do we handle this? By understanding the root cause:

Abusers were also abused in their past.

Put simply, we need to forgive our abusers. Jesus Christ loves them and died for them.

We need to thank God for the challenge of being abused because it gets us ready to make God our dad.

We need to flip the pain over into knowing God used it to mold our characters.

We need to remember that we are all a part of a Fallen Race. Pain results for all of us.

And we know that for those who love God all things work together for good, for those who are called according to his purpose.

—Romans 8:28

So What Do You Think?

_____

_____

_____

_____

_____

_____

_____

_____

_____

_____

_____

_____

_____

_____

_____

_____

_____

_____

_____

_____

_____

God is Lonely Without YOU!

But the Lord God called to the man and said to him, "Where are you?"
—Genesis 3:9

And I, when I am lifted up from the earth, will draw all people to myself.
—John 12:32

...Where I am you may be also.
—John 14:3

Abide in me, and I in you...
—John 15:4

I am my beloved's, and his desire is for me.
—Song of Solomon 7:10

Throughout Scripture, we can see how anxious God has been through the ages to draw people to Himself. We see this in the Commandments:

You shall have no other gods before me...I the Lord your God am a jealous God.
—Exodus 20:3, 5

What is He jealous about? He is jealous when we worship someone or something more than Him: "Thou shalt have no other gods before Me!" He wants you and me all to Himself.

Why? He has myriads of angels who worship Him, so why seek you and me? The Trinity created man to have fellowship, companionship, intimacy and a daily walk with us.

Why? I think it may be because He is lonely. Yes, I wonder if the Trinity is lonely without you and me. How humbling this thought is and how very precious—to think that I can make Him happy today by my worship, love and devotion.

How little we really know the Need our Lord has to be loved, believed, adored and worshipped. The whole Story of Calvary is for us to be reunited with our Maker. Sin separated us all from His Holy Presence, but Jesus Christ came and paid such a heavy price to restore us to Himself.

He hung on that cross totally exposed, nothing hidden, there was no cloth. His message to us was *"I am totally yours, I give myself to you completely…so take me into your life."*

What a precious thought, to think that He waits for me to love, worship and adore Him each day. Join me in doing this today!

So What Do You Think?

_____

_____

_____

_____

_____

_____

_____

_____

_____

_____

_____

_____

_____

_____

_____

_____

_____

_____

_____

_____

_____

Originals from Eleanor

Faith, Hope, and Love

Faith, Hope and Love always go together. Hope sets the Goal, Faith goes and gets it, and Love continues it all.

> So now faith, hope, and love abide, these three; but the greatest of these is love.
>
> —1 Corinthians 13:13

Triumph

It's never over, until I triumph in Christ! God causes us ALWAYS to triumph through Christ.

> I can do all things through Christ who strengthens me.
>
> —Philippians 4:13

Evil Unbelief

An evil heart is really the only sin that keeps us all from His Blessings. Unbelief is in the spirit.

> Take care, brothers, lest there be in any of you an evil, unbelieving heart, leading you to fall away from the living God.
>
> —Hebrews 3:12

Steam and Vapor

Our lives may be but a vapor, but when given to God can accomplish great things. Steam, when it is channeled, can pull a locomotive.

> Yet you do not know what tomorrow will bring. What is your life? For you are a mist that appears for a little time and then vanishes.
>
> —James 4:14

Creation

"Creation" is mentioned in Genesis 1:1—"God Created"—and so it remains. Not until Pentecost is the word used again—"Created in Christ Jesus."

In the beginning God created the heavens and the earth.

—Genesis 1:1

For we are his workmanship, created in Christ Jesus for good works, which God prepared beforehand, that we should walk in them.

—Ephesians 2:10

God's Supply

God has such a great storehouse for us that He needs to create a need in our lives so we can see we are lacking what He has. His supply is first, then comes the trial and testing to help us receive it!

Name of Jesus

In Psalm 119, we can substitute all the words: Statutes, Word, Testimonies, Precepts, Way, Commandments, Judgments, Righteousness, Law, and use the Name of Jesus in their place.

I have stored up Jesus (your word) in my heart, that I might not sin against you.

—Psalm 119:11

An Heir

We are not a sub-heir, but a Joint-Heir.

...We are children of God, and if children, then heirs—heirs of God and fellow heirs with Christ, provided we suffer with him in order that we may also be glorified with him.

—Romans 8:16-17

Obey

Don't pray when you need to obey!

Youth

The Lord is forever young. Strong. Victorious. Mighty. These are all energies of a young person.

Rahab

She ran a house of shame, yet became a part of the "Hall of Fame" (Joshua 2) and was one of Jesus' ancestors (Matthew 1:5).

The Ten Commandments

God keeps all of them in His relationship with you and me—how wonderful!

Shout

Our Lord Jesus shouted at least three times in the New Testament:

- At Lazarus' tomb (John 11:43)
- At the Cross (Matthew 27:46)
- When he returns (1 Thessalonians 4:16).

Kingdom

Thy Kingdom come? That means my Kingdom, my goals, plans and patterns will have to go!

366

There are 366 "Fear Nots" in the Bible. One for every day of the year, including Leap Year!

Enjoy

Enjoy yourself—these are the "good old days" you will miss ten years from now.

The Devil

When you give the Devil an inch He will become a "Ruler!"

A Person

When God wants to bless you, He will send you a person. Satan does the same thing if he wants to destroy you. So choose your friends wisely!

Early Bird

The early bird gets the worm. The early bird also gets the Word and the Blessing for the day!

Tragedy

Never judge a Tragedy on the day it happens!

The Answers

Christ is the Way. The answers to life's problems are not ON the way, but IN the Way!

> Jesus said to him, "I am the way, and the truth, and the life. No one comes to the Father except through me."
>
> —John 14:6

Pray

"Pray" is a four letter word which can be used anywhere!

Impatience

Whenever we are impatient with God's will for us, we create an Ishmael.

God's Eyes

God watches us all the time. He just can't take His eyes off of us - He loves us so much!

Book of Lamentations

This book is very sad, but it is in this book that we read "Great is Thy Faithfulness!"

The steadfast love of the Lord never ceases. His mercies never come to an end. They are new every morning. Great is your faithfulness.

—Lamentations 3:22-23

The Unknown

We don't really fear the unknown. We fear losing the known!

Tongues

We have three tongues—one in our mouth and two in our shoes. We should use all three to speak and walk the love of God wherever we go.

Halloween

Halloween is Satan's annual holiday. We get a glimpse of what hell will be like—death, destruction, no love, darkness, deception, scary, people who don't know each other, demons, abuse, fear, gruesome faces, phony laughter etc.

Samson

Weak in faith, victims of people and circumstances? Sometimes we act like Samson who has just been to the Barber! (Judges 16:7-22).

Sir Winston Churchill

Here are some of my favorite quotes from Sir Winston Churchill. Churchill as Prime Minister was instrumental in spearheading the United Kingdom's resistance to Nazi Germany during World War II.

Fear is a Reaction. Courage is a decision.

If you're going through hell, keep going.

A nation that forgets its past has no future.

—Sir Winston Churchill (1874-1965)

And my favorite quote of Churchill's that he didn't actually say:

Never give up. Never give up. Never give up.

This quote was altered from a longer speech Churchill gave at Harrow School for boys in London England in 1941. But really I like the shorter version better!

The Ocean

The ocean is like the Word of God—shallow enough for kids to play in at the edges, yet so deep that it is unfathomable!

Wings of Faith

Spread wide your wings of faith and soar on God's promises over your mountains of difficulty!

Shoes Did Not Wear Out

Did you ever think about this odd fact: while God let Moses lead the Jews in the wilderness for forty years—their shoes did not wear out? So... the shoes grew as the feet of the children grew. This to me IS the miracle.

I have led you forty years in the wilderness. Your clothes have not worn out on you, and your sandals have not worn off your feet.

—Deuteronomy 29:5

Virtue Going Too Far

When we take virtue too far, it can become a disaster. For example: Honor your mother and father too much? You will have no marriage. Devote yourself to your kids too much? You will have no life.

Goals and Processes

We seek goals but God seeks processes. We seek an end in a situation, but to God the process *is* the End!

Six Hours

God worked six days at Creation and six hours at our Redemption at Jesus' trials before Pilate and Herod, and the Cross of Calvary.

Choice

We can choose our sins, but we can't choose our consequences.

Powerful Friends

If God were not my friend, Satan would not be so great an enemy.

Welcome Home

Those who have welcomed Christ into their lives can joyfully welcome death.

So What Do You Think?

_____

_____

_____

_____

_____

_____

_____

_____

_____

_____

_____

_____

_____

_____

_____

_____

_____

_____

_____

_____

We Are Gifts to Jesus from the Father

[Jesus prayed] Since you have given me authority over all flesh, to give eternal life to all whom you have given me...I have manifested your name to the people *whom you gave me out of the world.* Yours they were, and *you gave them to me,* and they have kept your word...I am praying for them. I am not praying for the world but for *those whom you have given me,* for they are yours...And I am no longer in the world, but they are in the world, and I am coming to you. Holy Father, keep them in your name, *which you have given me,* that they may be one, even as we are one. While I was with them, I kept them in your name, *which you have given me.* I have guarded them, and not one of them has been lost except the son of destruction, that the Scripture might be fulfilled...Father, I desire that they also, *whom you have given me,* may be with me where I am, to see my glory that you have given me because you loved me before the foundation of the world.

— John 17:2, 6, 9, 11, 12, 24
emphasis added

For God so loved the world that he gave his only begotten Son, that whoever believes in him shall not perish but have eternal life.

—John 3:16

By this we know love, that he laid down his life for us, and we ought to lay down our lives for the brothers.

—1 John 3:16

How wonderful that Jesus considers every one of us a gift from the Father. That should certainly lift our spirits to greater heights and help us rise out of any feelings of depression and worthlessness.

John 3:16 tells us what Jesus Christ has done for us.

1 John 3:16 tells us what we now need to do for one another.

Let's look at all people as gifts, and treat them as having infinite value. After all, Jesus died for them, and called them his own.

So What Do You Think?

God is my Perfect Husband in Every Way
My Personal Testimony

For your Maker is your husband, the Lord of hosts is his name; and the Holy One of Israel is your Redeemer, the God of the whole earth he is called.

—Isaiah 54:5

I have been widowed for many years and the Lord has proven Himself in every way that He is my husband.

One morning before I got out of bed and looking out the window, I saw that we had had a big snow storm during the night. I thought, "*Oh no, how will I get out?*" You see, our backyard in this Retirement Community was being paved and no one could park their cars near the building. My car had to be parked in a different parking lot quite a ways from where I live.

As I snuggled up again under the covers, I said, "Now Lord, good husbands clean snow off their wives' cars. You say you are my husband. So what will you do, my heavenly husband?"

Let us then with confidence draw near to the throne of grace, that we may receive mercy and find grace to help in time of need.

—Hebrews 4:16

I am God's bride/wife and obey Him. I have learned to pray as a confident bride/wife and not as a baby does—gimme, gimme, gimme! I ask Him to take care of a need. No whining or begging, just plain FAITH, like a wife would ask her husband.

I got up, took care of my dog and went about doing my morning chores, actually forgetting what I said to the Lord while still in bed. I also decided that I would just stay home and not even think of going out. I drive an SUV and can't reach to the top of it.

Well, about an hour or so into the morning, I received a phone call from management.

"Mrs. Isaacson, we apologize that you cannot park your car behind your building because we are paving it and you've had to park so far away. So as a courtesy, I am calling you to let you know that we will clean off your car."

Talk about a quick answer to prayer!

Lord, you are terrific. Thanks so much for taking care of my car today, and for taking such wonderful care of me, in every way.

...Ask, and you will receive, that your joy may be full.

—John 16:24

So What Do You Think?

_____

_____

_____

_____

_____

_____

_____

_____

_____

_____

_____

_____

_____

_____

_____

_____

_____

_____

_____

God Doesn't Get Bored

What has been is what will be, and what has been done is what will be done, and there is nothing new under the sun.

—Ecclesiastes 1:9

I have seen everything that is done under the sun, and behold, all is vanity and a striving after wind.

—Ecclesiastes 1:14

It has always amazed me that God never gets bored with us or with what is happening in the world. Let's face it, nothing is ever new under the sun. People in every generation mess up their lives in the same way. There are no new sins under the sun. It is the same old, same old. The sins of Adam, Eve, and Cain still exist today.

The answers are always the same too—repent, believe, be baptized, and step over into God's way of living. If you walk in the Spirit then you will not fulfill the lust of the flesh.

How do we walk in the Spirit? Think about it this way: Remove the "H" from the word FLESH and you will get "self" spelled backwards. So walking in the flesh just means doing everything for self, and this is the backwards way to go.

But I say, walk by the Spirit, and you will not gratify the desires of the flesh.

—Galatians 5:16

So why doesn't God get bored?

It is because He is gracious, loving, forgiving, and He knows that we are dust. He is not willing that any should perish but that all should come to the knowledge of the Truth.

For he knows our frame; he remembers that we are dust.

—Psalm 103:14

...[The Lord] is patient toward you, not wishing that any should perish, but that all should reach repentance.

—2 Peter 3:9

So What Do You Think?

_____

_____

_____

_____

_____

_____

_____

_____

_____

_____

_____

_____

_____

_____

_____

_____

_____

_____

_____

Embracing the Ocean's Ebb and Flow
Life is that Way!

Or who shut in the sea with doors when it burst out from the womb ... and said, "Thus far shall you come, and no farther, and here shall your proud waves be stayed?"

—Job 38:8, 11

Your way was through the sea, your path through the great waters; yet your footprints were unseen.

—Psalm 77:19

You rule the raging of the sea. When its waves rise, you still them.

—Psalm 89:9

Who has measured the waters in the hollow of his hand and marked off the heavens with a span, enclosed the dust of the earth in a measure and weighed the mountains in scales and the hills in a balance?

—Isaiah 40:12

Thus says the Lord, who makes a way in the sea, a path in the mighty waters.

—Isaiah 43:16

And Jesus awoke and rebuked the wind and said to the sea, "Peace! Be still!" And the wind ceased, and there was a great calm.

—Mark 4:39

God is in control of the sea, its ebb and flow, and so is He in control of our lives! It is when we know and have experienced the Love of God for us that we don't drown under the waves.

So What Do You Think?

_____

_____

_____

_____

_____

_____

_____

_____

_____

_____

_____

_____

_____

_____

_____

_____

_____

_____

_____

The Tide is In

Oh how wonderful! Our lives are full of the blessings of the Lord. Our children obey us and family members are well, healthy and love us. Our marriages are satisfying and moving forward, our bank accounts are growing, our jobs are fulfilling, and our co-workers are all in harmony with one another. Even the weather seems to be perfect every day. Our own health seems to be perfect and our bodies are functioning perfectly—moving effortlessly and nothing hurts.

But this is for a season.

Tides are controlled by gravity, both of the moon and sun pulling at the waters in the Sea. The earth is constantly turning, and the pull of gravity affects different places as each day goes by. High tide occurs every 12 hours. God is definitely a mathematician. This universe is operating on a precise pattern, designed by our Creator.

The time is coming when the tide is out! So what do we do then?

So What Do You Think?

The Tide is Out

Suddenly, our lives are changed! Nothing seems to be going right for us and we question God's love for us. Author Kelli Stuart wrote "We can lament the unpredictability of it all, or we can jump into the waters and choose to enjoy each hectic, frightening, rushing of the waves and enjoy the exhilarating, exciting and beautiful moment." When waves of sorrow, disappointments and setbacks crash down on you, just pick yourself up and get ready for the next one.

Ride it like you own it!

So feel the kiss of the dancing waves and let your soul fly away with the seagulls into the heart of God who controls it all in your life. It is all for "a season." So many chapters in the Bible begin with *and it came to pass*... So it is with our lives.

Interesting though that the dry times in our lives are usually the most productive in building trust, surrender, and more time spent in the Word. We learn to abandon ourselves to the will of God and, yes, riding the waves of the storm. Our attitude speeds up the great calm of God.

So What Do You Think?

_____

_____

_____

_____

_____

_____

_____

_____

_____

_____

_____

_____

_____

_____

_____

_____

_____

_____

_____

Two Poems by Amy Carmichael

Amy Carmichael was an Irish Christian missionary to India. She founded an orphanage and worked and wrote tirelessly until her death in India at the age of 83.

The Tide is Out

Low lie the dank sea-weeds. The life is gone
That gave them strength to rise; and now forlorn
Low from the rocks they lie, waiting in patience
for the morrow morn,
When strong with life, and high, the tide will come in.

Far out at sea I watch the dancing waves
Rising to meet the seagull, as she leaves
in them her weary breast,
Fearless of all, the elements she braves,
seeking like me for rest, her tide is never in.

Low lifeless like the sea weed, now I lie.
Wishing that, like the gull, I swift could fly
from 'neath the burning sun
And scorching sands, that make me long to die,
Fearing that I am one
Whose tide will never come in.

Sinking upon the sand with bended knee
The cruel sand that soon will bury me
Unless the tide will soon come in;
With humble heart, Father, I pray to Thee,
Cleanse me from grief and sin
And make my tide come in!

—Amy Carmichael (1867-1951)

The Tide is In

Swift surging over the sand.
And now no more beside the barren,
Desolate sea shore I watch the sun dried rocks
And think my life like theirs is thirsting, sore
While cooling waters mock
For now the tide is in.

With grateful heart I lift mine eyes above
To Him who sent the tide, whose name is LOVE
Who saw me tired lie
In a strange land, like Noah's weary dove,
Not knowing He was nigh
Who makes the tide come in.

And lifting my drooped head, I now in haste
Go forth to meet my work, across the waste
Eager to live my life
As thou hast made it, Who gave me a taste
of weary care and strife
Before my tide came in.

So...the tide is in...but ah, the time will come
I know full well
That it will leave me; when, I cannot tell
But when that time shall come, I pray
That Thou my strong thoughts will quell
And take me to that home
Where tides are always in!

—Amy Carmichael (1867-1951)

So What Do You Think?

A Poem by Eleanor

My Bible
I am the Door to a Productive and Beautiful Life!

Hello, I am your Bible.
Don't keep me on the shelf!
I can teach you oh so many things
All about yourself!

When I'm opened up and read
I have so much to give.
I can share with you the Love of God
and show you how to live.

But God expects good things from you
So I must share that too.
Because He made you on your own
He knows what's best for you.

So pick me up and dust me off,
I am a special book.
Step here into my pages now,
Come take a closer look!

—Eleanor Isaacson

So What Do You Think?

_____

_____

_____

_____

_____

_____

_____

_____

_____

_____

_____

_____

_____

_____

_____

_____

_____

_____

_____

_____

_____

Just Think

I praise you, for I am fearfully and wonderfully made....

—Psalm 139:14

You are here not by chance, but by God's purpose and choosing! He has made you and formed you into the person you are and all your childhood joys and sorrows were a part of it all. This Psalm confirms this in the Bible—the World's Best Seller.

God compares you to no one else. You are one of a kind! You lack nothing that His Grace cannot give you today! So Trust Him! He has allowed you to be here at this time in history to fulfill His purpose for this generation. You have a very special mission.

So accept this today and have a great day trusting God to use you any way He chooses.

Just think how very special you are. Believe it!

—Author Unknown

So What Do You Think?

_____

_____

_____

_____

_____

_____

_____

_____

_____

_____

_____

_____

_____

_____

_____

_____

_____

_____

_____

_____

_____

_____

You are God's Valentine

For God so lo**V**ed the world.

That He g**A**ve

His on**L**y

Begott**E**n

So**N**

That whosoever

Believes **I**n Him

Shall **N**ot perish,

But have **E**verlasting life

—John 3:16

So What Do You Think?

_____

_____

_____

_____

_____

_____

_____

_____

_____

_____

_____

_____

_____

_____

_____

_____

_____

_____

_____

_____

_____

Reason to Live

YOU are my reason to live DEAR LORD
YOU are my hope through the day
YOU are my strength, when I'm tired and weak
YOU are there for me all the way

That's why my life is worth living
Though there be much testing and trial
Because I have YOU by my side, DEAR LORD
YOU are my reason to smile

YOU MIGHTY GOD, are my Counsellor
My Helper, my Hope, and my Friend
YOU give me peace, in the turmoil of life
YOUR angels around me YOU send

YOU speak to me by YOUR SPIRIT
YOU show me YOUR LOVE, day by day
YOUR faithfulness, truly astounds me
Should fear grip my heart LORD I pray

I know LORD, YOU always hear me
YOU'RE my Confidence, Peace, Joy and Calm
Because LORD YOU hold my life in YOUR hand
There never is need for alarm

YOU are my Lifetime Companion
I'm one with YOU LORD, that's for sure
Nothing can ever separate us
With YOU LORD, I shall endure

YOU are my reason to live SWEET LORD
Each day holds YOUR Blessings and Grace
And when my 'tomorrows' in this life shall end
In heaven, I'll see YOUR DEAR FACE
—By My Friend Lita Kurtzer

So What Do You Think?

Children and the Bible

...and how from childhood you have been acquainted with the sacred writings, which are able to make you wise for salvation through faith in Christ Jesus.

—2 Timothy 3:15

Train up a child in the way he should go: and when he is old, he will not depart from it.

—Proverbs 22:6

Children's children are the crown of old men; and the glory of children are their fathers.

—Proverbs 17:6

We can never underestimate the importance of children learning the Bible from the earliest days of their lives. Parents who are busy with the day to day activities should never neglect this invaluable part of family life!

Children are impressed when dad opens the Bible at the dinner table to read a verse. Little children may not understand the message, but the fact that Bible reading is a part of dinner will have a lasting impact on their lives.

Proverbs 22:6 tells us to *Train up a child in the way he should go: and when he is old, he will not depart from it.* He may slip away during his teens, but the influence his parents had in his childhood, regarding pursuing God and reading the Bible will encourage him to dwell and grow in his faith later in life. He will want to raise his children to know God when he becomes a parent. Parents may never see it, but they can rest assured that the Bible is true in this regard.

The crown of children is their fathers, especially when they are godly men and women and a strong example regarding the things of the Lord. "Oh my dad read the Bible to me at the dinner table and that shaped my life," they may say.

So my friends, please train up your children early in the way they should go. Give them a sure foundation of faith. It was St. Ignatius Loyola and later the Jesuits who said to parents of young children, "Give us a child until he is seven and we will have him for life!"

Your children will thank you for teaching them to pursue God as they grow into their adulthood.

So What Do You Think?

Pressed

Pressed out of measure and pressed to all length
Pressed so intensely it seems beyond strength

Pressed in the body and pressed in the soul
Pressed in the mind 'till the dark surges roll

Pressure by foes, and pressure by friends
Pressure on pressure, 'till life nearly ends

Pressed into loving the staff and the rod,
Pressed into knowing no helper but God

Pressed into liberty where nothing clings,
Pressed into faith for impossible things

Pressed into living a life in the Lord
Pressed into living a Christ-life outpoured!

It's Thy Hand, O Savior, that presses me sore
The Hand that bears the nail-print for evermore
And now beneath its shadow, hidden by Thee
The Pressure only tells...THOU LOVEST ME!

—Author Unknown

So What Do You Think?

_____
_____
_____
_____
_____
_____
_____
_____
_____
_____
_____
_____
_____
_____
_____
_____
_____
_____
_____
_____
_____

A Change in Names

Then he said, "Your name shall no longer be called Jacob, but Israel, for you have striven with God and with men, and have prevailed."

—Genesis 32:28

He strove with the angel and prevailed; he wept and sought his favor. He met God at Bethel, and there God spoke with us.

—Hosea 12:4

The study of the change in names in the Bible is a very interesting and fruitful one. Such a study reveals many thoughts and meanings which are not obvious to the casual reader.

Scholars are still divided on the meaning of the name "Israel," but the two Hebrew words of which it is composed mean "God-ruled." In other words, the word emphasizes being overcome by God rather than one who is an overcomer as is often thought.

If we had seen Jacob after that night of terrible, wrestling, we would not have thought of him as a conqueror. No, he was one who had allowed the Lord to conquer him!

> Make me a captive, Lord
> and then I shall be free;
>
> Force me to render up my sword,
> and I shall a conqueror be.
>
> —Don Hustad (1918-2013)

So What Do You Think?

Accept God's Ruling

...You have disciplined me, and I was disciplined, like an untrained calf; bring me back that I may be restored, for you are the Lord my God.

—Jeremiah 31:18

Come to me, all who labor and are heavy laden, and I will give you rest. Take my yoke upon you, and learn from me, for I am gentle and lowly in heart, and you will find rest for your souls. For my yoke is easy, and my burden is light.

—Matthew 11:28-30

It is only those who accept the Lord's ruling about things, who know how much joy there may be in little acts of self denial for His sake. Only those who are under the rule of God know how possible it is to be as free as a child in his Father's house.

It is only those who have taken upon themselves the yoke of Christ, who know how easy that yoke is. We who have taken it on know how free it makes them from all that irritates the spirit; how easily it rests upon our shoulders by reason of its soft lining of Love, and that it is only when we are under that yoke that we can find rest.

Draw me to Thee, 'till far within Thy rest
In stillness of Thy peace, Thy voice I hear
Forever quieted upon Thy breast
So loved, so near.

By mystery of Thy touch, my spirit thrilled
O Magnet all Divine,
The hunger of my heart forever stilled
For Thou art mine!

—Author Unknown

So What Do You Think?

_____
_____
_____
_____
_____
_____
_____
_____
_____
_____
_____
_____
_____
_____
_____
_____
_____
_____
_____
_____
_____

My Future

God holds the future in His Hand
Oh heart of mine, be still
His love will plan the best for thee,
The best, or light or dark it be
There rest thee in His Will

God holds the future in His Hand
Why should I shrink or fear?
Through every dark and cloudy day
Yea, all along my pilgrim way
His love will bless and cheer

God holds the future in His Hand
And I can trust His love
His past declares His faithfulness
His eye will guide, His heart will bless
'Till I am safe above

God holds the future in His Hand
I leave it all to Him
I know one day He will explain
The 'wherefore' of each grief and pain
Though reasons now are dim

—Author Unknown

So What Do You Think?

_____

_____

_____

_____

_____

_____

_____

_____

_____

_____

_____

_____

_____

_____

_____

_____

_____

Laid on the Altar of God

Even the sparrow finds a home, and the swallow a nest for herself, where she may lay her young, at your altars, O Lord of hosts, my King and my God.

—Psalm 84:3

That is the best place for our children to be—on the Altar of God!

So we see that sparrows and swallows lay their young on the Altar. How much we can learn from nature!

We worry, we struggle in prayer and sacrifice over our children. We work hard to bring them up "right," but all we really need to do is to give them to God, who gave them to us in the first place. Laying them on the Altar of God by faith is the best and safest place for them. That also means that when they become of age we need to "keep our hands off" the work of God in their lives.

So when they become adults, we must emphasize to them that they are now responsible for their actions and hopefully will remember everything we taught them as they were growing up under our care and discipline.

But when we do this, we must then accept everything that will come into their lives, joys and sorrows. We also must know that it is the dark times of their lives when spirituality is developed. We must not hinder the work of the Lord in their lives by stepping in repeatedly and inappropriately to ease well-deserved consequences of poor choices.

No, the work of God for all of us is to find Him in the dark times of a situation. We must be in the Word daily, eager and faithful to learn to rest in His Will for us.

Abraham did this in Genesis 22. He was one hundred, and his wife Sarah was ninety, when his boy Isaac finally arrived after more than twenty-five years of waiting. Of course it would be easy and natural for Abraham to absolutely adore, love, and almost worship his son.

I wonder if God may have become second in his life. Our God, being a jealous God (Deuteronomy 4:24), had to free Abraham from this idolatry.

God told Abraham to offer Isaac up as a burnt sacrifice on Mt. Moriah. He couldn't just let the knife "slip a little" on the boy's throat as he prepared the sacrifice. He had to kill him and burn him to a crisp!

Many people have a problem with this chapter. "How cruel God is," they say, "to ask such a terrible thing." Not so, my friend. God just wanted to free Abraham from his idolatry of this boy, Isaac, so that he could actually enjoy him more. Abraham enjoyed his son for many more years after this incident.

> And Abraham lifted up his eyes and looked, and behold, behind him was a ram, caught in a thicket by his horns. And Abraham went and took the ram and offered it up as a burnt offering instead of his son.
>
> —Genesis 22:13

Abraham clearly demonstrated that he was willing to give everything to God, even to give his son. And at the end of the story Abraham didn't have to kill Isaac because God provided a ram caught in the bushes for the sacrifice. Abraham had showed that God was first by faith. That is what God was after all along. Abraham was smart enough to obey!

> and in your offspring shall all the nations of the earth be blessed, because you have obeyed my voice.
>
> —Genesis 22:18

Isaac was the promised son and God had told him for many years that through him all the nations of the earth would be blessed. So

Abraham must have figured out that if God wanted him to kill this boy, then God would RAISE HIM FROM THE DEAD.

> But the angel of the Lord called to him from heaven and said, "Abraham, Abraham!" And he said, "Here I am." He said, "Do not lay your hand on the boy or do anything to him, for now I know that you fear God, seeing you have not withheld your son, your only son, from me."
>
> —Genesis 22:11-12

Sacrificing Isaac was a test! And Abraham passed it with flying colors. Let's all learn from this and obey God when a test like this comes across our paths. This chapter is also a foreshadowing of our Lord Jesus Christ, Who was willing to be our Sacrifice for sin.

So What Do You Think?

Two Different Seeds

[God speaking to Satan]. I will put enmity between you and the woman, and between your offspring and her offspring; he shall bruise your head, and you shall bruise his heel.

—Genesis 3:15

[God speaking to Abraham]. I will bless those who bless you, and him who dishonors you I will curse, and in you all the families of the earth shall be blessed.

—Genesis 12:3

[God speaking to David]. When your days are fulfilled and you lie down with your fathers, I will raise up your offspring after you, who shall come from your body, and I will establish his kingdom. He shall build a house for my name, and I will establish the throne of his kingdom forever.

—2 Samuel 7:12-13

The three prophesies mentioned above refer to three branches of the same seed:

- The Seed of the Woman.
- The Seed of Abraham.
- The Seed of David.

The seed finally narrows to one person—the Messiah, our Lord Jesus Christ!

- As the Seed of the woman, the Lord Jesus Christ is to be the Conqueror and Destroyer of Satan himself.
- As the Seed of Abraham, He is going to be the World's Blessed Redeemer.
- As the Seed of David He is to be the King—the One bringing Eternal Righteousness.

It's amazing how God used a thread of seed throughout many generations to bring it to completion.

So What Do You Think?

_____

_____

_____

_____

_____

_____

_____

_____

_____

_____

_____

_____

_____

_____

_____

_____

_____

_____

_____

_____

_____

_____

_____

His Plan for Me

When I stand at the judgment seat of Christ
And He shows me His plan for me,
The plan of my life as it might have been
Had He had His way....and I see—

How I blocked Him here, and I checked Him there
And I would not yield my will—
Will there be grief in my Savior's eyes,
Grief, though He loves me still?

He would have me rich, and I stand there poor,
Stripped of all but His grace,
While memory runs like a hunted thing
Down the paths I cannot retrace.

Then my desolate heart will well-nigh break
With the tears that I cannot shed;
I shall cover my face with my empty hands,
I shall bow my uncrowned head.

Lord of the years that are left to me
I give them to Thy hand;
Take me and break me, mould me to
The pattern Thou hast planned.

—Author Unknown

So What Do You Think?

_____

_____

_____

_____

_____

_____

_____

_____

_____

_____

_____

_____

_____

_____

_____

_____

_____

_____

_____

_____

_____

Footprints in the Sand

One night I had a dream.

I dreamed I was walking along the beach with the Lord, and across the sky flashed scenes from my life. For each scene, I noticed two sets of footprints in the sand. One belonging to me and the other to the Lord.

When the last scene of my life flashed before me, I looked back at the footprints in the sand. I noticed that many times along the path of my life, there was only one set of footprints. I also noticed that it happened at the very lowest and saddest times in my life. This really bothered me and I questioned the Lord about it.

"Lord, you said that once I decided to follow you, you would walk with me all the way, but I noticed that during the most troublesome times in my life, there was only one set of footprints. I don't understand why in times when I needed you most, you should leave me!"

The Lord replied, "My precious, precious child, I love you and I would never never leave you during your times of suffering. When you saw only one set of footprints, it was then that I carried you!"

—Mary Stevenson (1922-1999)

So What Do You Think?

Concealed Glory

Could there be a greater miracle than that You, Lord Jesus, was for only 30 years on this earth before You did any miracles?

We foolish people, if we have but a dream of virtue, we are impatient to show it off, but You were patient and wise enough to be content to live in willing obscurity, and conceal the power that made this world and us. You did not choose to live in a palace, but in a little cottage in Nazareth.

The stars are not seen by day and the sun itself is not seen by night. Your power and glory was not seen until the proper time and season.

It is no small glory to conceal glory!

—Author Unknown

So What Do You Think?

Jesus Christ

Both Masculine and Feminine Qualities

Jesus wept.

—John 11:35

Lazarus come forth.

—John 11:43

Jesus wept at the tomb of Lazarus because He was a close friend of the family and it was appropriate for Jesus to be sad. Here we see His humanness and gentleness—more traditionally feminine qualities. But when Jesus called his friend Lazarus to exit the grave, we see the Godhead demonstrating his power

Jesus throughout his ministry was both strong and gentle, powerful and compassionate. In him these two qualities were perfectly blended.

Strength is common in manhood and tenderness is a mark of womanhood. If we meet a woman who is strong, clever and goal-oriented, we might be a little taken aback. If we meet a man who is soft and tender, we may consider him weak and pity him. Aggressiveness and tenderness are seldom both consistently displayed in one person.

However, these characteristics of power and compassion are in perfect harmony in our Lord Jesus. First He wept at the grave of Lazarus showing His love, compassion and tenderness, and a few minutes later, He raised him from the dead, showing His strength, power and Glory.

Hallelujah, what a Savior we have.

So What Do You Think?

_____

_____

_____

_____

_____

_____

_____

_____

_____

_____

_____

_____

_____

_____

_____

_____

_____

_____

_____

Thy Father's Will for You

Not in thy way, my child, thy blessing I intend,
A portion undefiled, and not with time to end;
Pure links with an eternal love
That neither life nor death can move

Not in thy time, dear one, the joys that thou
has sought; Thou wouldst the grief have known
Untimely joys had brought
Oh, wait my time, and waiting prove
True joys in my eternal love

For in my time and way doth lie thy truest gain;
Nor shall it pass away, but evermore remain;
For I, thy Father, love thee, child,
And all I give is undefiled

Have not I kept thy tears, heard even thine inward cry?
And who has waited on thy fears so tenderly as I?
My sorrowing child, thou yet shalt stand
To bless thy Father's love and chastening hand

Dear one, then seek to prove how much thou art to me
For with an everlasting love, thy Father loveth thee
Heart of my child, oh, then be still, thy blessings are
in thy Father's Will

—Author Unknown

So What Do You Think?

_____

_____

_____

_____

_____

_____

_____

_____

_____

_____

_____

_____

_____

_____

_____

_____

_____

_____

_____

Earthly and Heavenly Contrasts

Yes, there are beautiful and interesting contrasts and seeming contradictions in the Bible. "Oh no," people say. "The Bible is perfect and there are no contradictions in it at all." I agree. But God in His word contrasts the earthly with the heavenly, or the human with the divine! Let's delve into this concept. So come with me...

Enlarged Heart and Running

I will run in the way of your commandments when you enlarge my heart!
—Psalm 119:32

People with an enlarged heart don't run in races. An enlarged heart reduces the ability to do physical work.

Of course, in this context an "enlarged heart" probably refers to an emotional heart that is able to expand with love for God.

Corruptible Gold versus Blood

...knowing that you were ransomed from the futile ways inherited from your forefathers, not with perishable things such as silver or gold, but with the precious blood of Christ, like that of a lamb without blemish or spot.
—1 Peter 1:18-19

We were not redeemed with corruptible things as silver and gold, but with the precious blood of Christ!

Although silver may tarnish, gold and silver don't ever corrupt which makes them precious metals. Blood however starts changing and degrading the minute it hits the air. If you bleed from cutting your finger, you can't put the blood back into the body because it has started to clot.

But the Precious Blood of Christ shed for our sins is to God incorruptible. What a contrast.

Losing and Gaining

> For whoever would save his life will lose it, but whoever loses his life for my sake…will save it.
>
> —Mark 8:35

Humanly speaking this is an obvious contrast. We don't gain anything by losing it. But not so with the Lord. If we want to have a meaningful life, we must give it up for the Lord to use, and we will find fulfillment in our lives

Rich and Poor

> One pretends to be rich, yet has nothing; another pretends to be poor, yet has great wealth.
>
> —Proverbs 13:7

> Do not toil to acquire wealth...
>
> —Proverbs 23:4

In the world, we labor and save to be rich, but in the spiritual true riches are not tangible but spiritual. If God blesses you with wealth, it is for you to give it to help others. To be rich, give it all away.

Life and Death

> Truly, truly, I say to you, unless a grain of wheat falls into the earth and dies, it remains alone; but if it dies, it bears much fruit.
>
> —John 12:24

Humanly speaking, we think of death as the end. But our Lord Jesus says just the opposite. To produce fruit in our lives we must die to our own plans, purposes and goals. It is when we totally surrender to the Will of God for our lives that we bear much fruit for Him.

So What Do You Think?

_____

_____

_____

_____

_____

_____

_____

_____

_____

_____

_____

_____

_____

_____

_____

_____

_____

_____

_____

_____

_____

_____

Brokenness

There is a boy here who has five barley loaves and two fish, but what are they for so many?

—John 6:9

But Jesus said to them, "You give them something to eat." They said, "We have no more than five loaves and two fish—unless we are to go and buy food for all these people." For there were about five thousand men.

And Jesus said to his disciples, "Have them sit down in groups of about fifty each." And they did so, and had them all sit down.

And taking the five loaves and the two fish, Jesus looked up to heaven and said a blessing over them. Then he broke the loaves and gave them to the disciples to set before the crowd.

And they all ate and were satisfied. And what was left over was picked up, twelve baskets of broken pieces.

—Luke 9:13-17

The people were blessed and so were His disciples after the loaves were BROKEN. Notice that the disciples were also blessed and fed, having twelve baskets leftover and full for them.

It is when we are broken of getting our own will, broken of our self esteem, broken of our plans and goals, broken of all the things that we are proud of in ourselves that God can really use us and we become a blessing to many, and we are blessed as well.

There are many examples in the Word of God of people receiving the blessing of being broken and then used. Look them up in your Concordance:

- Joseph—favorite son of his father, he was sold into slavery before rising to second of command in Egypt and saving many people from starvation. (Genesis 37-Genesis 50).

- Moses—raised in the Pharaoh's family, he was thrown out of Egypt and became an obscure shepherd in a foreign land before he led the Jewish people toward the Promised Land. (Exodus).

- David—shepherd boy anointed as king by Samuel after Saul, he was brought down by sin in acquiring his wife Bathsheba, and later withstood attempts to unseat him as king by his own son Absalom before returning to the joy of the Lord. (1 Samuel, 2 Samuel, 1 Kings 1-2).

- Paul—a merciless persecutor of the believers of Jesus, he met Christ on the road to Damascus and became a powerful preacher and writer of much of the New Testament. (Acts).

How wonderful that God gives us people in the Bible to help us cope with our own brokenness. So when we are broken ourselves, let's thank God for the pain because we know that He has a purpose in mind for our growth and service.

> And I am sure of this, that he who began a good work in you will bring it to completion at the day of Jesus Christ.
>
> —Philippians 1:6

> It is good for me that I was afflicted, that I might learn your statutes.
>
> —Psalm 119:71

> ...My son, do not regard lightly the discipline of the Lord, nor be weary when reproved by him. For the Lord disciplines the one he loves, and chastises every son whom he receives.
>
> —Hebrews 12:5-6

So we can all rest in His promises that when the trial is over, we will be a blessing not only in becoming more thankful to our Lord for the brokenness, but looking back we see that we are more useful in serving others.

So What Do You Think?

In God's Furnace

When God wants to drill a man and thrill a man and skill a man.
When God wants to mold a man,
To play the noblest part;

When He yearns with all His heart to create so great and bold a man
That all the world shall be amazed,
Watch His methods, watch His ways;

How He ruthlessly perfects, whom He royally elects:
How He hammers him and hurts him,
And with mighty blows converts him

Into trial shapes of clay which only God understands;
While His tortured heart is crying
And he lifts beseeching hands!

How He bends but never breaks, when his good He undertakes;
How He uses whom He chooses,
And with every purpose fuses him;

By every act induces him, to try His splendor out —
God knows what He's about!

The Christian life is a quarry out of which
God molds and chisels a beautiful character!

—Author Unknown

So What Do You Think?

_____

_____

_____

_____

_____

_____

_____

_____

_____

_____

_____

_____

_____

_____

_____

_____

_____

_____

_____

_____

Pulled Out

I would have pulled Joseph out. Out of that pit, out of that prison, out of that pain. And I would have cheated nations out of the one God would use to deliver them from famine.

I would have pulled David out. Out of Saul's spear-throwing presence. Out of the caves he hid away in, out of the pain of rejection, and I would have cheated Israel out of a God-hearted king.

I would have pulled Esther out, out of being snatched from her only family. Out of being placed in a position she never asked for. Out of the path of a vicious, power-hungry foe. And I would have cheated a people out of the woman God would use to save their very lives.

And I would have pulled our Lord Jesus Christ off, off the cross, off the road that led to suffering and pain, off of the path that would mean nakedness and beatings, nails and thorns. And I would have cheated the entire world out of a Savior, out of salvation and out of an eternity filled with no more suffering and no more pain!

And oh my friend, I want to pull you out. I want to change your path, I want to stop your pain. But right now I know I would be doing the wrong thing. I would be out of line. I would be cheating you and cheating the world out of so much good. Because God knows, He knows the good this pain will produce. He knows the beauty this will develop in you. He is watching over you and keeping you even in the midst of all this in your life. And He's promising you that you can trust Him, even when it all feels like more than you can bear.

So instead of trying to pull you out, I'm lifting you up! I'm kneeling before the Father and I'm asking Him to give you strength. To give you hope and I'm asking Him to protect you and to change things when the time is right. I'm asking Him to help you stay prayerful and discerning and I'm asking Him how I can best love you and help you.

I am believing that He will use your life in a powerful and beautiful way, ways that will leave your heart grateful and humbly thankful for this road you are on today.

—Kimberley Henderson
Proverbs 31 Ministries

So What Do You Think?

Born a Woman

...[She] brought an alabaster flask of ointment, and standing behind him at his feet, weeping, she began to wet his feet with her tears and wiped them with the hair of her head and kissed his feet and anointed them with the ointment.

—Luke 7:37-38

... Mary, who sat at the Lord's feet and listened to his teaching.

—Luke 10:39

I am glad I was born a woman! I can have a tender, intimate and quiet love relationship with our Lord Jesus even without saying a word. Throughout the four Gospels, it seems that the women quietly sat at His feet, heard His word and showed Him tenderness and devotion. We don't read anywhere in the Gospels that women argued with Jesus about anything. They just believed what He said, even about His death and resurrection. When Jesus was crucified they watched only from a distance:

There were also many women there, looking on from a distance, who had followed Jesus from Galilee, ministering to him,

—Matthew 27:55

There were also women looking on from a distance, among whom were Mary Magdalene, and Mary the mother of James the younger and of Joses, and Salome.

—Mark 15:40

... the women who had followed him from Galilee stood at a distance watching these things.

—Luke 23:49

> Standing by the cross of Jesus were his mother and his mother's sister, Mary the wife of Clopas, and Mary Magdalene.
>
> —John 19:25

The women just trusted Jesus and followed Him. The men, on the other hand, squabbled about who would be the greatest among them and questioned things Jesus told them.

> At that time the disciples came to Jesus, saying, "Who is the greatest in the kingdom of heaven?"
>
> —Matthew 18:1

> … And Peter took Jesus aside and began to rebuke him. But turning and seeing his disciples, Jesus rebuked Peter and said, "Get behind me, Satan! For you are not setting your mind on the things of God, but on the things of man."
>
> —Mark 8:32-33

The men tried to manage things and often came to Jesus only as a last resort. They were men of action. Peter even wanted to build three tabernacles on the Mountain of Transfiguration:

> …Peter said to Jesus, "Master, it is good that we are here. Let us make three tents, one for you and one for Moses and one for Elijah."…
>
> —Luke 9:33

However, not all the men mentioned in the Gospel argued with the Lord. Nicodemus and Joseph of Arimathea (members of the Jewish ruling body the Sanhedrin) loved the Lord silently. After the crucifixion they claimed Jesus' body from Pilate provided the embalming spices to prepare the body of Jesus for burial.

So [Nicodemus and Joseph of Arimathea] took the body of Jesus and bound it in linen cloths with the spices, as is the burial custom of the Jews. Now in the place where he was crucified there was a garden, and in the garden a new tomb in which no one had yet been laid. So because of the Jewish day of Preparation, since the tomb was close at hand, they laid Jesus there.

—John 19:40-42

Then there was John, the disciple whom Jesus loved. John leaned against Jesus at supper.

Now there was leaning on Jesus' side one of his disciples, whom Jesus loved.

—John 13:23

But generally speaking, it was the women who brought Jesus comfort, love and acceptance.

This doesn't make women superior. No, but perhaps just more emotional, loving and tender.

So What Do You Think?

Made in God's Image

So God created man in his own image, in the image of God he created him; male and female he created them.

—Genesis 1:27

The oral messages of the creation story and patriarchs were first written down, probably by Moses who was educated in the finest schools of Egypt. As the Israelis continued to live in their land more stories and instructions were written by other scribes. The writings were handed down from generation to generation.

Did the people in the Old Testament really know what it meant to be made in God's Image? So many of the writers in the Old Testament imagined God to be a man with a body like ours.

The Eyes of the Lord

The eyes of the Lord are toward the righteous and his ears toward their cry.

—Psalm 34:15

The Ears of the Lord

...for you have wept in the ears of the Lord...

—Numbers 11:18

The Nose of the Lord

Smoke went up from his nostrils, and devouring fire from his mouth; glowing coals flamed forth from him.

—Psalm 18:8

The Mouth of the Lord

...man does not live by bread alone, but man lives by every word that comes from the mouth of the Lord.

—Deuteronomy 8:3

The Face of the Lord

You have said, "Seek my face." My heart says to you, "Your face, Lord, do I seek."

—Psalm 27:8

The Mind of the Lord

...that the mind of the Lord might be showed them.

—Leviticus 24:12

The Heart of the Lord

...the Lord has sought out a man after his own heart...

—1 Samuel 13:14

The Arm of the Lord

...To whom has the arm of the Lord been revealed?

—Isaiah 53:1

The Hand of the Lord

Behold, the hand of the Lord...

—Exodus 9:3

The Finger of God

... This is the finger of God...

—Exodus 8:19

The Feet of the Lord

...His way is in whirlwind and storm, and the clouds are the dust of his feet.

—Nahum 1:3

The Footsteps of the Lord

Your way was through the sea, your path through the great waters; yet your footprints were unseen.

—Psalm 77:19

With the coming of our Lord Jesus Christ, we have seen the fullness of God in His Person.

His mouth is most sweet, and he is altogether desirable. This is my beloved and this is my friend, O daughters of Jerusalem.

—Song of Solomon 5:16

So What Do You Think?

Assurance

I will keep thee; simply trust Me all the way
Through the desert I will guide thee day by day

Child, the pathway thou art treading I have trod
And, despite the trials thou art dreading leads to God!

When the tempest rises round thee, trust Me still
Through the storm I'll gently bear thee; fear no ill

When the night is dark, remember I am Light;
Fix thine eyes upon the beacon, shining bright.

When thou art weary with thy pathway, seek my face
I will give thee for the journey needed grace.

All the way, I will be with thee; thou shalt prove
That the ways of God are simply endless love!

—Author Unknown

So What Do You Think?

A Trip to the Country

One day, the father of a very wealthy family took his son on a trip to the country with a firm purpose of showing his son how poor people can live.

The son spent a couple of days and nights on the farm of what would be considered a very poor family. On his return, the father asked his son, "How was the trip, my son?"

"It was great, Dad," the boy said. "Thanks!"

"Did you see how poor people can be?" The father asked.

"Oh yeah," said the son.

"So what did you learn from the trip?" asked the father.

The son answered:

"I saw that we have one dog and they have four dogs. We have a pool that reaches to the middle of our garden and they just have a creek that has no end. We have imported lanterns in our garden and they just have stars at night. Our patio reaches in the front yard and they have the whole horizon. We have a small piece of land to live on and they have fields that go beyond our sight. We have servants who serve us all day every day but they serve others. We buy our food in many stores or it's delivered to us but they grow theirs.

"We have walls around our property to protect us and they have friends and God to protect them. We don't have time for God or prayer or going to church but they pray before each meal.

"We are independent and don't have a need for God. They are thankful and praise God all the time. We are really not happy or grateful people but fearful. These people trust in God and have no care."

With this, the boy's father was speechless. He was angry and disappointed.

But as he thought about it, he realized he'd learned more than his son about his son's visit with the poor people.

—Verna & Viola Mueller

The Mueller twins Verna and Viola, now in their late 80s, grow flowers for their Willow Street PA business, *Mueller Twins Flowers*. In their community they love to present faith-based programs that use flower arrangements to illustrate Bible verses.

So What Do You Think?

Waiting on God

The Lord is good to those who wait for him, to the soul who seeks him. It is good that one should wait quietly for the salvation of the Lord.
—Lamentation 3:25-26

It is easier to work than to wait! It is often more important to wait than to work. We can trust God to do the needed working while we are waiting, but if we are not willing to wait, and insist upon working while He would have us be still, we may interfere with the effective and triumphant working that He would do on our behalf. Our waiting may be the most difficult thing we can do. It may be the severest test that God can give us.

Truly one of the greatest strains in life is the strain of waiting for God. God takes a believer like a bow which He stretches; we get to a certain point and say "I can't stand it any more!" But God goes on stretching. He is not aiming at our mark, but at His own and the patience of the believer is that we hold on until He lets the arrow fly straight to His goal.

If we are willing to remember God's call and assurance, there need be no strain at all while we are waiting. The stretched bow time may be a time of unbroken rest for us as we rest in the Lord and wait patiently for Him.

—Oswald Chambers (1874-1917)

Be still before the Lord and wait patiently for him; fret not yourself over the one who prospers in his way, over the man who carries out evil devices!

—Psalm 37:7

Unless a violin string is stretched until it cries out when the bow is drawn over it, there is no music. A loose violin string with no strain upon it is of no use—it Is dead. But when stretched until it strains, it is brought to the proper tone, and then only is it useful to the musician.

In God's eternal plan, a month, a year is but an hour of some slow April day, holding the seeds of what we hope for to blossom far away.

—Andrew Murray (1828-1917)

Our God is tough and gentle at the same time. He is ruthless in shaping all of us into a useful instrument—to be like Christ!

So What Do You Think?

Only Wait

Oft there comes a gentle whisper o'er me stealing
When my trials and my burdens seem too great

Like the sweet-voiced bells of evening softly pleading,
It is saying to my spirit, only wait.

When I cannot understand my Father's leading
And it seems that life is hard and cruel fate

Still I hear that gentle whisper ever pleading
God is working, God is faithful, only wait!

When the promise seems to linger, long delaying
And I tremble lest, perhaps, it comes too late,

Still I hear that sweet-voiced angel always saying
Though it tarry, it is coming, only wait.

When I see the wicked prosper in their sinning
And the righteous pressed by many cruel straits,

I remember that is only the beginning
And I whisper to my spirit, only wait

Oh, how little soon will seem our hardest sorrow
And how trifling is our present brief estate

Could we see it in the light of heaven's tomorrow
Oh, how easy it would be for us to wait!

— Author Unknown

Lead me in your truth and teach me, for you are the God of my salvation;
for you I wait all the day long.

—Psalm 25:5

So What Do You Think?

The Gospel in a Song

He saved us, not because of works done by us in righteousness, but according to his own mercy…

—Titus 3:5

Not What My Hands Have Done

Not what my hands have done can save my guilty soul
Not what my toiling flesh has borne can make my spirit whole
Not what I feel or do can give me peace with God
Not all my prayers, sighs and tears can bear my awful load.

Thy work alone, O Christ, can ease this weight of sin,
Thy blood alone, O Lamb of God, can give me peace within
Thy love to me, O God, not mine, O Lord, to thee
Can rid me of this dark unrest, and set my spirit free.

Thy grace alone, O God, to me can pardon speak
Thy power alone, O Son of God, can this sore bondage break
No other work, save thine, no other blood will do;
No strength, save that which is divine, can bear me safely through

I bless the Christ of God, I rest on love divine
And with unfaltering lip and heart, I call this Savior mine
His cross dispels each doubt, I bury in His tomb
Each thought of unbelief and fear, each lingering shade of gloom

I praise the God of grace, I trust His truth and might
He calls me His, I call Him mine, my God, my joy my light
'Tis He who saves me, and freely pardon gives
I love because He loves me, I live because He lives

—Horatius Boner (1808-1889)

124

For by grace you have been saved through faith. And this is not your own doing; it is the gift of God, not a result of works, so that no one may boast.

—Ephesians 2:8-9

Salvation is a gift from God, but we must open the gift and receive it into our lives. If You have never done this, my friend, don't put it off—do it today!

So What Do You Think?

The Gospel of John
Chapters 3 and 4

John Chapter 3	John Chapter 4
Old Testament	New Testament
Jesus talks to a religious man (Nicodemus)	Jesus talks to the woman at the well (Samaritan woman)
Nicodemus is Jewish	The Samaritan woman is Gentile
Jesus speaks of earthly things	Jesus speaks of heavenly things
Nicodemus is an upright man	The Samaritan woman is an immoral woman
Nicodemus came to Jesus by night	Jesus came to the Samaritan woman at noon
Nicodemus sought out Jesus	The Samaritan woman was sought out by Jesus
Jesus talks about Nicodemus	Jesus talks about himself
Water during visit is used for washing	Water during visit is used for drinking
External cleansing	Internal cleansing
Water in the basin is confined	Water in the well springs up into eternal life
No mention of worship	Worship God in Spirit and Truth

Old Testament foreshadows the cross	New Testament begins at the cross
Jesus talked in 3rd person	Jesus said, "I am He."

It is interesting to compare and contrast when studying the Scriptures. So my friend, look for things like this in your Bible study and see what a rich blessing the Lord has for you.

So What Do You Think?

God is Waiting on Us

Therefore the Lord waits to be gracious to you...blessed are all those who wait for him.

—Isaiah 30:18

We must not only think of our waiting upon God, but also of—more wonderful still—God waiting on us!

The vision of Him waiting upon us will give new impulse and inspiration to our waiting on Him. It will give us confidence that our waiting is not in vain. God has wonderful and glorious purposes for every one of His children.

So you may ask, "How is it that if He waits to be gracious, that even after I come and wait on Him, He does not give the help I seek but waits on longer and longer?"

God is a wise husbandman, father, guide, who waits for the precious fruit of the earth, and has long patience for it. He cannot gather the fruit until it is ripe. He knows when we are spiritually ready to receive the blessing to our profit and His Glory.

Waiting in the sunshine of His love is what will ripen the soul for His blessings. Waiting under the cloud of trial, that breaks in showers of blessings, is what is needed on our part.

Be assured, that if God waits longer than you could wish, it is only to make the blessing more precious to you!

God waited four-thousand years until the fullness of time, before He sent His son, our Lord Jesus Christ. He will make haste for our help and not delay one hour too long

—Andrew Murray (1828-1917)

So my friend....wait, trust and love Him who only wants the very best for you! Remember, God is not obligated to pay all his bills on Tuesday!

So What Do You Think?

_____

_____

_____

_____

_____

_____

_____

_____

_____

_____

_____

_____

_____

_____

_____

_____

_____

_____

_____

_____

_____

_____

Bored with Jesus?

And the people spoke against God and against Moses, "Why have you brought us up out of Egypt to die in the wilderness? For there is no food and no water, and we loathe this worthless food."

—Numbers 21:5

I am the living bread that came down from heaven. If anyone eats of this bread, he will live forever...

—John 6: 51

The bread, manna, which came down from heaven is a type of our Lord Jesus.

Can we ever get bored with Him? Yes—it's called "backsliding." We can get bored with all that love, joy and peace He gives us.

In the Old Testament, God sent manna—bread from heaven—to the Israelites every day for forty years while they were wandering in the wilderness on their way to the Promised Land. God provided bread and water faithfully, but the Israleites got bored with it all and started blaming God and Moses for their boredom.

In the New Testament, we read that our Lord Jesus Christ is the Bread of Life, who came down from heaven. We see that the Old Testament story about the Israelites in the desert (described in the book of Numbers) is a type, a foreshadowing of the coming of Christ, the Messiah, the True Bread from heaven.

So the Israelites got bored with it all. I call that backsliding! Backsliding is just another way of saying, "I'm bored with Jesus and all that joy and peace He gives me." WOW!

Believers who think that way usually walk away from the Lord because they want some excitement the world can offer. They believe Satan's lies. They don't realize that the consequences of walking away from the Lord are costly. When their lives begin to fall apart, they blame God, the preachers, the churches and their friends for their problems.

God is faithful and will begin the restoration process for a backslider. It may take years of suffering, guilt, shame and everything else Satan puts in front of them, but it can happen. Sadly though some people never get back to the Lord. They become bitter and resentful and think that God is unfair. There are many backsliders who die while still being angry and resentful for the consequences of not making God first in their lives. They forget that the direction that their lives went was their choosing.

However, once a restored believer has seen his error and come back to the Lord, he is more committed to the Lord and His service than he was before he left. There is true repentance of such a one and they don't want to backslide again. We see this in the lives of many leaders in the Bible such as Moses and David in the Old Testament, and Peter in the New.

So my friend, if you identify with wanting to find a new way, be encouraged that God is working diligently to restore you to Himself. Use your mistakes as a stepping stone to a richer and more productive walk with the Lord.

So What Do You Think?

Permanent Forgiveness

Then Peter came up and said to him, "Lord, how often will my brother sin against me, and I forgive him? As many as seven times?" Jesus said to him, "I do not say to you seven times, but seventy-seven times."

—Matthew 18:21-22

Are you struggling with making forgiveness "really stick?"

So you have been hurt, abused, neglected and abandoned as a child and you try to forgive, now that you have become a Christian and know that "you should forgive." But it just keeps coming back into your mind and heart and you feel hurt all over again. You have tried everything to forgive these toxic people but you are helpless with it.

Let's face it. We all have had toxic people in our paths, people that we just can't stand, but we either have had them in our families when we were growing up or we are stuck now working with some of them. Worse yet, you may be married to one of these creatures.

I have been through this wilderness…in and out….but finally the Lord has shown me the answer and I want to share it with you now.

If you have made the Lord Jesus Christ, not only your Savior, but also your Lord and have really meant business with Him, remember, He now owns you. He has bought you with His own blood on the cross of Calvary. That means that you now belong to Him. You are no longer your own!

When we give up ownership of our lives and let God direct our events and use us any way He wishes, He first has to crush us, hurt us, throw us into a furnace to take away the dross—like pride, arrogance, our will, our plans and goals, our self esteem and our self-made accomplishments. That hurts! Before He can use any of us, we need to be broken of all that. So how is God going to accomplish that?

By bringing very toxic people into your life to force you to look to Him, to let Him mold you, soften you, trust Him to make it all work out for good in your life.

And we know that for those who love God all things work together for good, for those who are called according to his purpose.
—Romans 8:28

Whenever God wants to force us to grow, He will usually send you a Person. Satan will do that too if he wants to destroy you.

We read our Bibles more eagerly when we are hurting. King David said it well:

Before I was afflicted I went astray, but now I keep your word.
—Psalm 119:67

And Jeremiah talks about us being clay to be molded:

...Can I not do with you as this potter has done? declares the Lord. Behold, like the clay in the potter's hand, so are you in my hand...
—Jeremiah 18:6

When we know that we have a very loving Father who is the one molding us into a useful vessel, we can just hold still under His Hand. We know that He has a purpose for it all.

The only way I have found to make a forgiveness "stick" is to thank God for those toxic people to help me focus on Him.

Forgiveness is the fragrance we send out to the heel that crushed us.
—Mark Twain (1835-1910)

So What Do You Think?

God is Weaving Our Lives

My life is but a weaving between my God and me
I may not choose the colors,
He knows what they should be

For He can view the pattern upon the upper side
While I can see it only
On this, the under side

Sometimes He weaves sorrow which seems strange to me
But I will trust His judgment
and work on faithfully

'Tis He who fills the shuttle, He knows just what is best
So I shall weave in earnest
and leave with Him the rest

At last, when life is ended, with Him I shall abide
Then I may view the pattern
Upon the upper side

Then I shall know the reason why pain with joy entwined
Was woven in the fabric of life that God designed!

—Corrie Ten Boom (1892-1983)

Corrie Ten Boom probably wrote this while she was in Hitler's Concentration Camp. What a testimony that woman had for all of us.

So What Do You Think?

Eleanor Isaacson

Ten Steps to Breaking Bondages

1 Know your enemy—the Devil

Your enemy is not your husband or wife, parents, boss, kids, or siblings. Your enemy is not people. Your enemy is a spiritual enemy.

For we do not wrestle against flesh and blood, but against the rulers, against the authorities, against the cosmic powers over this present darkness, against the spiritual forces of evil in the heavenly places.
—Ephesians 6:12

2 Know that your battle is won by faith

Believe the Bible. We are all on the winning side. Jesus said so. All authority is His and we are in Him.

And Jesus came and said to them, "All authority in heaven and on earth has been given to me."
—Matthew 28:18

3 Know that God promises to help us

So if your faith has sprung a leak in your situation, plug it up with promises in your Bible and believe the promises.

And those who know your name put their trust in you, for you, O Lord, have not forsaken those who seek you.
—Psalm 9:10

4 Words of unbelief are death

Think and speak words of faith. Words of faith have power. They are our most powerful tool. So change your thoughts and words, and God's power will change your life.

Death and life are in the power of the tongue, and those who love it will eat its fruits.
—Proverbs 18:21

5 Claim your God-given place

Believe and claim what is yours in knowing Jesus Christ! Notice that our inheritance is all in the past tense. It all has your name on it. So take hold of it in your situation and move forward with the Lord.

In him we have obtained an inheritance, having been predestined according to the purpose of him who works all things according to the counsel of his will.

—Ephesians 1:11

6 Believe God will hear you

Pray believing that God hears your prayers and will answer them in His time.

And if we know that he hears us in whatever we ask, we know that we have the requests that we have asked of him.

—I John 5:15

7 Know that God will fight for you

Stand upon God's promises in faith and strength. It is His battle, not yours.

You will not need to fight in this battle. Stand firm, hold your position, and see the salvation of the Lord on your behalf... Do not be afraid and do not be dismayed. Tomorrow go out against them, and the Lord will be with you...And the fear of God came on all the kingdoms of the countries when they heard that the Lord had fought against the enemies of Israel.

—2 Chronicles 20:17, 29

8 You receive a new name

God changes your name when you become His. You can see this phenomenon recorded in the Bible:

- Abram to Abraham, meaning "father of many nations" (Genesis 17:5).
- Sarai to Sarah, meaning "princess" (Genesis 17:15).
- Jacob to Israel, meaning "struggle with God and God prevails" (Genesis 32:28).
- Saul to Paul, meaning "chosen vessel" (Acts 9:15).
- Simon to Peter, meaning "the rock" (Matthew 16:18).

9 We still do things wrong

Even after we belong to God, we can and do still sin against Him. Many in the Bible, including Tamar, Moses, Jonah, Samson, David, Peter, and Paul, committed great sin because they didn't believe God, and only later repented.

King David is a great example of someone who didn't keep his eyes on God. David broke at least half of the Ten Commandments: lying to a priest (1 Samuel 21:1-2), coveting his neighbor's wife (2 Samuel 11:2-3), adultery (Samuel 11:2-4), murder (2 Samuel 11:15-17), and then stealing his neighbor's wife (2 Samuel 11:27).

David messed up his life but he repented. Thankfully we can do the same.

If we say we have no sin, we deceive ourselves, and the truth is not in us. But if we confess our sins, he is faithful and just to forgive us our sins and to cleanse us from all unrighteousness.

—1 John 1:8-9

10 Even though we sin, we sin less

The important thing to remember is that, as we grow closer to God, *we sin less*. You don't just say "I'm forgiven" and do all the bad things you used to do. You notice that your life is looking cleaner!

Therefore, if anyone is in Christ, he is a new creation. The old has passed away; behold, the new has come.

—2 Corinthians 5:17

And be careful—if you see that your life isn't much different than it was before you became a Christian, or not much different from the non-Christians around you, you should ask yourself if you really are following Jesus the way he wants you to.

> Then Jesus told his disciples, "If anyone would come after me, let him deny himself and take up his cross and follow me."
>
> —Matthew 16:24

> For if we go on sinning deliberately after receiving the knowledge of the truth, there no longer remains a sacrifice for sins.
>
> —Hebrews 10:26

So my friend, there is hope for all of us. Sometimes when we fail, we realize how very human and frail we all are. This makes us love our Lord Jesus Christ even more.

So What Do You Think?

_____

_____

_____

_____

_____

_____

_____

_____

_____

_____

_____

_____

_____

_____

_____

_____

_____

_____

_____

_____

_____

_____

_____

_____

How to Handle Fear

For God gave us a spirit not of fear but of power and love and self-control.
—2 Timothy 1:7

Believe it not, we are born with just two fears—the fear of noise and the fear of falling. All other fears are learned, which means we can unlearn them if we want to. How about that?

So what really is fear? We fear the unknown. We are insecure about what to do in a situation. We fear being alone. If we don't enjoy a solid love relationship with the Lord, fear will dominate our lives.

The opposite of fear is not courage, strength or experience, but it is love, the love of God! When we know that we are so loved by the Lord, then all things are possible. We are loved by the Lord Jesus Christ who paid such a price to make us His. The Father loves us who planned our redemption by sending His son to die for us. The Holy Spirit, who now lives inside of us, loves us and helps our shortcomings. We are loved by the Trinity for all eternity. So why fear anything or anyone?

Fear is a spirit but we now have the Holy Spirit within us to give us the victory in all situations. We need to believe the love God has for us. It is a choice on our part. Choose love today and don't fear.

We love him because he first loved us.
—1 John 4:19

There is no fear in love, but perfect love casts out fear...
—1 John 4:18

The fear of God is a fountain of life...
—Proverbs 14:27

...the Lord shall give you rest from your sorrow, and from your fear...

—Isaiah 14:3

...My heart shall not fear...

—Psalm 27:3

Fear not, for I am with you....

—Isaiah 43:5

...In God I trust. I shall not be afraid...

—Psalm 56:4

The Lord is on my side; I will not fear. What can man do to me?

—Psalm 118:6

So my friend, when fear knocks on your door, don't put on the coffee and get ready to have a conversation with him! (haha)

To handle fear positively, let it be a stepping stone to faith. Decide to trust the Lord and deny yourself. Do not allow yourself to become a victim of fear.

So What Do You Think?

_____

_____

_____

_____

_____

_____

_____

_____

_____

_____

_____

_____

_____

_____

_____

_____

_____

_____

_____

_____

_____

Widowhood

He executes justice for the fatherless and the widow, and loves the stranger, giving him food and clothing.

—Deuteronomy 10:18

Father of the fatherless and protector of widows is God in his holy habitation.

—Psalm 68:5

...and let your widows trust in me.

—Jeremiah 49:11

God took your mate because He wanted you all to Himself! Looking at it this way will ease the pain of your loss!

There is a life for us after we walk away from a cemetery and a covered grave. It is a new life now, only different!

Psychologists tell us that widowhood is the most serious and stressful time in our lives. Our identity was being someone's mate. Suddenly, we are one in a world of twos. It can make us into a whole new person, with new goals, new activities, serving our church and community and becoming a spiritual person.

So how can we handle it all in a positive way? First, we allow a period of grief. We carry tissue boxes around with us, and pull out all the old photos, the wedding album, and the honeymoon souvenirs. We stare at the photos and remember the good old times. We go to the closet and touch all the clothes of our loved one and have some good crying moments. This is all normal. However we can't choose to live in that mode forever. There has to come a time when we say to ourselves "Enough!"

I hope you have a personal relationship with the Lord. If you don't, now would be a good time to do that by opening your heart to the Lord Jesus Christ, who bought you with His own blood on Calvary's cross. He is now your present husband (or wife). Trust Him to guide you into a new life. Let it all make you a spiritual person.

Double up on your prayer time and really study and believe the Bible daily. No Bible—No Breakfast! is a good rule to start your day with.

Don't make it a habit to always run to people and Family for comfort. No—pray and speak to God about it. God's Holy Spirit will help you.

Some helpful hints to help you move forward:

- You must eat well every day. Ditch the junk food and go easy on sweets and coffee.
- Drink lots of water upon rising.
- Find new single people and plan trips or dinners.
- Make new goals as a single person. Rearrange the furniture especially in your bedroom. Take some college courses. Join clubs, a church, prayer groups, and book clubs. Write your own story. Go on vacations with yourself.
- Become active in your community. Entertain people in your home for coffee or start a widows' group. Read to seniors in retirement places, join an art class or a theater group. Volunteer at the hospital or the soup kitchen to help those less fortunate than you.
- Definitely exercise daily. Walk often and take a nap if you have to.
- Think happy thoughts—it's a good habit.

Grief and pain can become a "sacred dance" as God turns pain into passion. Thank God all the time, even for the pain and emptiness. He will fill it! Forgive people in your past, move forward with God and remember that the Best is yet to be in your new life in heaven!

So What Do You Think?

Vibrant Senior

So even to old age and gray hairs, O God, do not forsake me, until I proclaim your might to another generation, your power to all those to come.

—Psalm 71:18

They are planted in the house of the Lord; they flourish in the courts of our God. They still bear fruit in old age...

—Psalm 92:13-14

And even to your old age I am he, and to gray hairs I will carry you. I have made, and I will bear; I will carry and will save.

—Isaiah 46:4

What wonderful promises from our God to seniors. Some of the most productive years are the senior years, depending on how you lived getting there! So you think your life is over once you have blown out seventy candles on your birthday cake? You feel you have come to the last gas station in life? Well my friend, just refuel and keep on keeping on! It's all about attitude! I am no longer a teen-ager, but a seen-ager, and now I have everything I wanted only fifty years later!

- I don't have to go to school anymore unless I want to.
- I get an allowance every month—not from my dad, but from Uncle Sam.
- I don't have curfews. I can come and go whenever I want.

Brains of older people are slow because they know so much. And all this information in the brain puts pressure on the ears so hard of hearing is the result.

But it is all great and wonderful!

What you can do…

Read a book a week, watch less TV, be open to new adventures, go to college—its free—work puzzles or write your life story for your children and grandchildren.

Always put God first in all you do, and be thankful and grateful for every day of your life. You are so loved by God—believe it!

Maintain a good posture, be well groomed at all times even when you are home alone, walk a mile a day, eat frequent smaller meals, be outgoing, continue dreaming of your future, and get rid of anything that isn't useful, beautiful or gives you joy!

All that really matters in the end is that you are loved by God. Nothing is more important!

So What Do You Think?

_____

_____

_____

_____

_____

_____

_____

_____

_____

_____

_____

_____

_____

_____

_____

_____

_____

_____

_____

_____

_____

_____

More Thoughts from Eleanor

The Lion

...Behold, the Lion of the tribe of Judah...

—Revelation 5:5

...You would hunt me like a lion...

—Job 10:16

Our Lord Jesus Christ is the Lion of the Tribe of Judah. When a lion chases after its prey, he is bound to get it! So Jesus, the Lion of the tribe of Judah, chased after me and got me. Praise God.

Worship

Worship is what God really wants from all of us more than any service we can do for Him.

Fire

Beloved, do not be surprised at the fiery trial when it comes upon you to test you, as though something strange were happening to you.

—1 Peter 4:12

The fire makes the beauty permanent. Without the fire, a vessel is too fragile to be used. The fire is what is needed to make it useable, permanent and strong. Our lives are to be burning embers, not ashes.

Prison

The word of the Lord came to Jeremiah while he was shut up in the court of the guard, saying "Go, and say to Ebed-melech the Ethiopian, 'Thus says the Lord of hosts...'"

—Jeremiah 39:15-16

How can Jeremiah go and speak when he is shut up in prison? Good question. He is to go by faith! He needed to think through everything and be ready so that when the doors opened he was all ready to speak.

So with us! We are not to settle into our prison, whatever that may be, but we are to believe and receive the promises that God is using it for us to stretch our faith in Him. We need to work it all out for His Glory and our good!

> And we know that for those who love God all things work together for good, for those who are called according to his purpose.
>
> —Romans 8:28

Believing

> The Lord is my shepherd; I shall not want.
> He makes me lie down in green pastures. He leads me beside still waters.
> He restores my soul. He leads me in paths of righteousness for his name's sake.
> Even though I walk through the valley of the shadow of death, I will fear no evil, for you are with me; your rod and your staff, they comfort me.
> You prepare a table before me in the presence of my enemies; you anoint my head with oil; my cup overflows.
> Surely goodness and mercy shall follow me all the days of my life, and I shall dwell in the house of the Lord forever.
>
> —Psalm 23

There is a difference between believing IN God and believing ABOUT God! Believing IN God is to enjoy all His promises every day! So don't pick and choose the promises—they are all yours.

Soul and Spirit

Soul love is emotion. Spirit love is will.

Favorites

God has no favorite kids, but He does have intimates!

Darkness

For God, who said, "Let light shine out of darkness," has shone in our hearts to give the light of the knowledge of the glory of God in the face of Jesus Christ.

—2 Corinthians 4:6

The light shone OUT of the darkness, not INTO the darkness. The Lord was IN the darkness waiting for the right time to shine forth. Times of darkness in our lives are to be the backdrop for the "diamond" you are!

Solitude

To become a person of purpose it is absolutely necessary to have spiritual growth. Jesus Christ is our example. To be unique, one must welcome solitude and loneliness.

Near

When you think He doesn't hear….He is always near.

Care

People don't care how much you know! Until they know how much you care.

Journey

The longest journey is to…. within.

Treasures

Just think of the treasures that lie at the other side of our obedience

Dash

Our lives are really just a dash on our tomb stone, a space between our birth and death. But it can mean a lot for whatever we do now for eternity. It has been said:

Only one life, 'twill soon be past,
only what's done for Christ will last!

—C.T. Studd (1860-1931)

A Victim

I am never a victim of any situation if I take up my responsibility immediately and don't accept defeat. A victim mode has no solution!

God's Heart

God's heart sings when we seriously pursue Him.

Self-Pity

Did you ever stop to think that self pity is really Satan's babysitter? He can stop bothering you. He can work on somebody else. He already accomplished what he planned to do with you. Interesting isn't it?

Suffering

He said, "Take your son, your only son Isaac, whom you love, and go to the land of Moriah, and offer him there as a burnt offering on one of the mountains of which I shall tell you."

—Genesis 22:2

The Father probably suffered more at Calvary than did Jesus Christ.

Abraham suffered more than his son Isaac on the Mt. of Moriah, when he obeyed the Lord to offer up his son. Isaac knew nothing about what went on in the heart of Abraham. This story is a foreshadowing of our Lord Jesus, who was willing to be offered as our substitute on the cross of Calvary.

Home

Even as he chose us in him before the foundation of the world, that we should be holy and blameless before him. In love he predestined us for adoption to himself as sons through Jesus Christ, according to the purpose of his will.

—Ephesians 1:4-5

What does "home" really mean? It means it is a place where we have been before. So when we say our loved one has "gone home to be with the Lord" we mean that in the heart of God, our loved one was always there. Each time we pray and appear before the throne of the Lord, we are really coming home too.

Be Ready

When you are ready, the teacher will appear!

Pray and Act

Pray as if it all depends on God; act as if it all depends on you!

Rejected at Home

Then Samuel said to Jesse, "Are all your sons here?" And he said, "There remains yet the youngest, but behold, he is keeping the sheep." And Samuel said to Jesse, "Send and get him, for we will not sit down till he comes here."

—1 Samuel 16:11

David had four giants in his life: Jesse his father, Elliab his brother, Saul the king, and Goliath, the giant. David knew who he was in God.

For Jesse, when Samuel wanted to anoint one of his sons as king it was probably one of the most important events in Jesse's life. Yet, he forgot to call David, his youngest son. who was keeping the sheep in the field. David was not considered worthy to be present by his father. How could he do that?

Great Leaders

It is interesting to note that many of the great leaders mentioned in the Bible were rejected. It was this rejection that forced them all to turn to the Lord for strength, courage, and confidence. Think about it: Joseph who was sold as a slave and imprisoned became the second in command of the most powerful nation at that time and saved many from starvation. Moses who ran away from a crime and lived in obscurity led the nation of Israel out of Egypt. David who was a shepherd boy, became a king and "a man after God's own heart" (1

Samuel 13:14). So, if you want to be a great leader, remember you need to be humble and not be intimidated by rejection.

God a Consuming Fire

Why is hell so hot? Because if we don't embrace and receive God's passion of love, we will have to receive His passion of hot wrath. How wonderful that God's love for us is so consuming that we should never be discouraged about anything that comes into our path. Are you feeling lukewarm or cold to God? Just cuddle up with Him. He is a consuming fire of love.

The Throne or the Phone?

Which one do we run to in a crisis? Putting God first in everything is the way we need to act. It is a simple choice, but a powerful one!

Tree

A tree can only be measured when it is down. It is then that we see the circles of life on the inside. So it is with us. How do we act when we are down? Our faith can be measured by the way we handle our down times.

Thank God for Friends

> Thank God for friends upon our earthly journey,
> To travel with and make life's journey sweet.
>
> For those who have 'like precious faith' and gather
> Together with us 'round the Master's feet'.
>
> Thank God for friends whose love exceeds our failures,
> Whose understanding reaches past the blame;
>
> Whose friendship thrives alike on sun and shadow
> With golden glow and warmth - a steady flame.

Thank God for friends whose loving prayers uphold us
When trouble comes and we're too weak to cry.

How sweet it is to know when we're just clinging
To Him alone, our friends are standing by!

Thank God for friends whose faith in us surpasses
Each whispered doubt whose kindness never ends.

Oh may we each day prove more worthy of them
This golden gift from God, our Christian friends.

—Alice H. Mortenson (1898-1988)

So What Do You Think?

The Gospel Story in Psalm 119

I am the Alpha and the Omega, the first and the last, the beginning and the end.

—Revelation 22:13

This interesting and unusual Psalm has 176 verses with 22 subdivisions. Psalm 119 celebrates the Jewish New Year with "Yamim Nora'im"—the Days of Awe, found in God's Word. Its theme is to learn and celebrate God's Word. It is read by Jewish Rabbis every year on the Jewish New Year—Rosh Hashanah.

Psalm 119 is the longest Psalm but it can also be considered the longest personal prayer. It is known as the "Everest of the Psalms." Each verse in each stanza begins with the same letter of alphabet. For example, each line of the eight verses in the first stanza begin with Aleph, the Hebrew letter "A." This Psalm is used not only to learn the Hebrew alphabet but also to learn the formula for a spiritual life.

Psalm 119 shows us the attributes of God throughout the Psalm: Righteousness, Truth, Trustworthy, Purity, Light, Eternal, Unchanging, Faithfulness, and Loving. When you are reading this psalm you may want to substitute "Jesus" for the words: Law, Testimonies, Word, Precepts, Statues, Commandments, Judgments and Ordinances. It will make these laws not only more personal but very inspiring and beautiful.

So how does this Psalm tell us the Gospel Story in a nutshell?

The heading of the first section begins with Aleph. The last section—22—ends with Tau. Aleph means "Ox" and Tau means "Cross." These brackets seem to perfectly describe the sacrifice of our Lord Jesus Christ who, like an ox in the Old Testament, was offered as a sin sacrifice on the Cross of Calvary. (Hebrews 9:12).

It is so wonderful to study the Bible in depth. What riches are hidden there for us not only to enjoy our faith but also to worship our Lord in greater adoration of who He is.

When our Lord Jesus Christ was walking among us for thirty-three years, He never quoted from this Psalm. It is really all about the Word. Jesus Christ is the Living Word. Maybe that is why He didn't quote from it.

So What Do You Think?

The First Adam and the Last Adam

So God created man in His own image...

—Genesis 1:27

For to us a child is born, to us a son is given...

—Isaiah 9:6

Adam was created a full grown man, but our Lord Jesus Christ was born an infant and became a man.

Adam never had to grow up. He had no idea what it was like to be a boy, with all its disciplines and experiences that go with it. Could this be a part of the reason why he was a bad influence on his son, Cain? Was he unable to train up his son in the way he should go so that when he is old, he will not depart from it, like we read in the book of Proverbs chapter 22:6? So why should Cain do what was right in the sight of the Lord? He just followed in his father's footsteps! After all, Adam sinned and disobeyed the Lord, so why should Cain obey?

Who knows if Adam had any authority in that family anyway. Eve seemed to be in charge right from the start. She may have trained the children 'not to take all that God stuff so seriously'. That is what she did. She took from the tree of the knowledge of good and evil and gave also to Adam. He should have known better, but was weak and so sinned against the Lord. Adam is really to blame. It was God who gave Adam the command not to eat of that tree. We are all born into his family, sinners. We are all of a fallen race because of it.

However, our Lord Jesus Christ, having been born and growing up in favor with God and man, knew what childhood was all about. He is therefore able to be our perfect Savior, both to children and adults. He showed us how to grow up in favor with God and man also. He is our perfect example.

In Christ we are a new creation created in Christ Jesus (2 Corinthians 5:17) because He is the Last Adam, the Second Man, to be the head of a new race. He did no sin. Unlike Adam who was the first Adam. Therefore Christ could pay for our sins on the cross of Calvary to restore the human race to a relationship with God. Hallelujah what a Savior we have, One Who knows our frame and remembers that we are dust (Psalm 103:14).

So What Do You Think?

Tradition or Christ?

And as he entered a village, he was met by ten lepers, who stood at a distance and lifted up their voices, saying, "Jesus, Master, have mercy on us." When he saw them he said to them, "Go and show yourselves to the priests." And as they went they were cleansed. Then one of them, when he saw that he was healed, turned back, praising God with a loud voice; and he fell on his face at Jesus' feet, giving him thanks. Now he was a Samaritan. Then Jesus answered, "Were not ten cleansed? Where are the nine? Was no one found to return and give praise to God except this foreigner?" And he said to him, "Rise and go your way; your faith has made you well."

— Luke 17:12-19

In Leviticus chapter 14, we read the law concerning the cleansing of a leper. These ten men who heard about our Lord Jesus lifted up their voices and pleated for mercy. They knew He could healed them and they also knew the law concerning their disease.

At the command of the Lord, the nine followed their tradition to go to the priest and present themselves. But one, who was not Jewish, was on his way to the priest also, but after he saw that he was healed, turned back to the Lord not only to thank Him but also to glorify God. He knew the deity of the Lord Jesus Christ.

He not only broke away from tradition to show himself to the priest, but he went to the Real Priest, the Lord Jesus Christ. The nine lepers were healed, but this man was made whole.

So my friend, are you following the traditions of your church and its doctrines? If that Church is in strict accordance to the Word of God, and you are growing strong in your faith, you are in the right place. Stay there and serve the Lord there. However if you are in the Word faithfully and begin to question their doctrine and lifestyle, you may want to really pray about it. If God shows you that the church you attend does not line up with the Word, are you bold enough to leave and just follow the Lord Jesus Christ and His Word? Ask yourself that question and it may surprise you how many doors God may open to you for your blessing and growth, if you leave and find another church.

So What Do You Think?

Food

So when the woman saw that the tree was good for food...

—Genesis 3:6

Did you every think about this? Sin came into this world through food!

It seems that in almost every book of the Bible, things happen good and bad over food.

It was at a banquet that Joseph revealed himself to his brothers in Genesis. In Exodus it was the Passover supper and in the wilderness it was the Manna that fell from heaven. Book of Numbers, tells us about how they brought back a branch of grapes from Eshcol.

In the book of Ruth, we read that Boaz fell in love with Ruth at the dinner table. King Saul was ready to throw his javelin at David at the dinner table in the book of 1 Samuel. Job received that terrible news about the death of his children while he was having dinner, and Esther saved the whole nation of Israel because she gave luncheons. In the book of Daniel, we see the handwriting on the wall at a banquet, and our Lord Jesus Christ in John 2, began His ministry at a wedding, when He turned water into wine. After His resurrection, He made breakfast on the beach and Peter jumped out of the boat to swim to Him to enjoy it. The little boy gave his lunch to the Lord and 5,000 men were fed plus women and children in Matthew. In Revelation we read of the Marriage supper of the Lamb and we don't read that the supper ever ends.

So food is an important part of our lives, and we must respect it and not let it rule us. There are many verses in the Bible about gluttony. Please look them up in your Concordance as your morning devotion, and you will see how controlling our food intake should be a part of our walk with the Lord. Our bodies are the temple of the Holy Ghost we read in 1 Corinthians 6:19, and in verse 10:31 we read... whether therefore you eat or drink, or whatsoever you do, do all to the glory of God.

So What Do You Think?

_____

_____

_____

_____

_____

_____

_____

_____

_____

_____

_____

_____

_____

_____

_____

_____

_____

_____

_____

_____

My Olde Order Amish Families

I was interviewed by a newspaper reporter, after my talk at a Sunday Church service, regarding my book *Dancing from Darkness*. The article appeared in the Sunday paper a week later, not only of the talk I gave about it, but with the pictures he took of my posters, myself and the book table filled with my books.

An Olde Order Amish Bishop read the article and called me saying that he and his family want to meet with me and the guest they were hosting in their home who was from Germany. We met and almost instantly I connected with them, speaking German and feeling so very at home with them. I was invited to their home to meet the family and help celebrate the Bishop's birthday the next day.

After cutting the cake, the Bishop asked me to talk about my times in Germany under the Hitler Regime, the bombings, starvation, invasions by the Americans and then Russians and finally coming to the United States alone at the age of 13.

Many of the guests had lots of questions about the war, and the Bishop said "Do you see that big barn behind you?" I turned around the said "yes."

Then he said, "Well, how would you like to give your talk in that barn if I get all my Amish neighbors together?"

Of course I said yes! And a few weeks later the event took place. After that many other Amish families asked me to speak in their barns as well.

This started a wonderful friendship and relationship with many Amish families with whom I am in touch almost on a weekly basis. My book opened the door and I am so delighted to spend time with many families. I really admire the Amish in so many ways. They live simple lives, close to nature and their vegetables gardens, and stress the importance of strong family ties and prayer at every meal. It has been said *the family that prays together stays together* and I believe it.

The Amish young people, beginning at age sixteen, meet in a youth group every Sunday evening and many of them meet their mates at these gatherings. They marry young and enjoy large families. They attend school only to the 8th grade and learn how to think and how to have a healthy family life as they get older and marry. There are almost no divorces in this community. They pray, forgive and move on with their lives if problems arise.

I thank God for having brought me into the Amish Community and I look forward to growing relationships with many of the Olde Order Amish people. I get invited to weddings, birthday parties, wedding and baby showers and funerals and I try to attend as many as I can. I am so impressed with the way the whole Community gathers around each other when there is a crisis.

I trust that the beauty of the Olde Order Amish Community lifestyle will never pass away. God bless the Amish people.

So What Do You Think?

About the Author

Born in New Jersey, speaker, author, and WWII survivor Eleanor Isaacson was raised till age thirteen in East Germany. Returning to the USA with neither English nor family, she overcame every obstacle to graduate with a double Bachelor's Degree magna cum laude, become a successful business entrepreneur, and marry renowned scientist Dr. Robert Isaacson. She is also a competitive ballroom dancer with more than 100 first-place wins.

Eleanor has been an inspirational speaker for more than forty years throughout the United States. She was voted "The Speaker of the Year" for the past five years in Lancaster County. She was also awarded an honorary Doctoral Degree from Lancaster Bible College in 2017.

You can contact Eleanor on her website at
www.eleanorisaacson.com.

Read Eleanor's Award-Winning Story!

Dancing from Darkness: A WWII Survivor's Journey to Light, Life, and Redemption

2018 Memoir of the Year by American Writers and Speakers Association

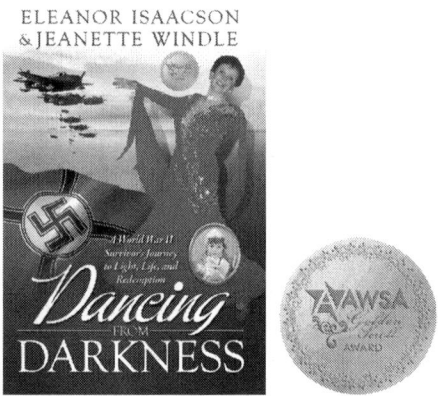

Abandoned as a toddler in Nazi Germany, American-born Eleanor Isaacson survived bombings, starvation, Russian occupation, and a stint as a child smuggler—all before reaching her teens.

Escaping just as the Iron Curtain clashed shut, Eleanor soon discovered that "the land of the free" held as much pain and rejection as the life she'd escaped. Deafness and solitude would become the catalyst leading to glorious womanhood, the love of her life, and the beauty of dance.

In the process, she would discover that the "invisible Friend" whose presence alone had kept a lost child sane had other names— heavenly Father, loving God, Prince of Peace.

A true story too implausible for fiction with every element of a big screen epic—war, danger, starvation, villains, romance, rags-to-riches triumph—along with the most delightful of heroines.

Another Book by Eleanor

The Invisible Presence: Meditations to Help You Praise, Pray, Think, and Smile

The Invisible Presence has its inception from Dr. Eleanor Isaacson's award-winning top-selling personal survival story *Dancing from Darkness*. Abandoned as a toddler in Nazi Germany, American-born Eleanor survived bombings, starvation, Russian occupation, and a stint as a child smuggler—all before reaching her teens. Throughout it was the Invisible Presence who made Himself known to her that kept a lost child sane. A Presence she would eventually come to know by other names—heavenly Father, loving God, Prince of Peace.

Since Eleanor began sharing her story, listeners and readers alike have begged to know more about her encounter with the Invisible Presence and how they too might find Him. Responding to those pleas, *The Invisible Presence* is a compilation of meditations and humorous thoughts on God, faith, Scripture, and Eleanor's own spiritual journey intended to make the reader praise, pray, think, and smile.

Invite Eleanor to Speak

As a presenter and confident speaker, Eleanor Isaacson is available to speak to various groups, including schools, on a variety of topics including:

- Finding God in Nazi Germany

- The Educational System under the Nazi Regime

- The Christmas Tradition—Why we Do It the Way We Do

- Positive Attitudes and Nutritional Helps that Can Help You to Be Your Best at Any Age

- How to Be a Vibrant Senior

- Widowhood—the Next Stage of the Adventure

- How to Break Generational Bondages—Dealing with Difficult Parents as an Adult

You can contact Eleanor on her website at
www.eleanorisaacson.com

Made in the USA
Middletown, DE
21 November 2021

52408026R00113